The Psychology of Demonization

Promoting Acceptance and Reducing Conflict

The Psychology of Demonization

Promoting Acceptance and Reducing Conflict

Nahi Alon & Haim Omer
Tel Aviv University

2006

LAWRENCE ERLBAUM ASSOCIATES, PUBLISHERS
Mahwah, New Jersey London

Lawrence Erlbaum Associates, Inc., Publishers
10 Industrial Avenue
Mahwah, New Jersey 07430
www.erlbaum.com

Cover design by Tomai Maridou

Library of Congress Cataloging-in-Publication Data

Alon, Nahi
The Psychology of Demonization : promoting acceptance and reducing conflict / Nahi Alon & Haim Omer.
p. cm.
Includes bibliographical references (p.).
ISBN 0-8058-5665-X (cloth : alk. Paper)
ISBN 0-8058-5666-8 (pbk. : alk. paper)
1. Psychotherapy—Case studies. 2. Interpersonal conflict—Case studies. 3. Demonic possession. I. Omer, Haim. II. Title.

RCA480.5.A46 2005
616.89'14—dc22 2005049829
CIP

Books published by Lawrence Erlbaum Associates are printed on acid-free paper, and their bindings are chosen for strength and durability.

Printed in the United States of America

10 9 8 7 6 5 4 3 2 1

Contents

Foreword

I believe that the purpose of life is to be happy. From the moment of birth, every human being wants happiness and does not want to suffer. Therefore, it is important to discover what will bring about the greatest degree of happiness.

The authors of this book are both psychotherapists, dealing professionally with people seeking help to find mental peace and satisfaction. They are concerned to make their work more effective. One of the psychotherapeutic trends they wish to challenge is the tendency toward what they call the demonization of things or people. Our normal tendency is to try to blame our problems on others, on external factors. Furthermore, we tend to look for one single cause, and then try to exonerate ourselves from responsibility. It seems that whenever intense emotions are involved, there tends to be a disparity between how things appear to us and how they really are. When we demonize people, we see them in a very negative light and pretend that they are somehow completely different from us.

We overlook the fact that all human beings are basically the same, wherever we come from. Physically, there may be a few small differences in the shape of our noses, the color of our hair and so on, but these are insignificant. Basically, we are the same. We all have the same potential to undergo both positive and negative experiences. What' s more, we also have the same potential to transform our attitudes. And this is what I think is important; to recognize that we can each transform ourselves into better, happier people. Not only that, we should also take strength from the thought that, if we can do it, our rivals, opponents, and enemies can change too.

From my own limited experience, I have found that the greatest degree of mental peace comes from the development of love and compassion. The more we care for the happiness of others, the greater our own sense of well-being becomes. Cultivating a close, warm-hearted feeling for others automatically puts the mind at ease. This helps remove whatever fears or insecurities we may have and gives us the strength to cope with any obstacles we encounter. This is why I believe it is the ultimate source of success in life.

In Tibet we have a saying: "Many illnesses can be cured by the one medicine of love and compassion." These qualities are the ultimate source of human happiness, and our need for them lies at the very core of our being. Unfortunately, love and compassion have been omitted from too many spheres of social interaction for too long. Confined to family and home, their practice in public life is considered impractical, even naive. This is tragic. In my view, the practice of compassion is not just a symptom of unrealistic idealism, but is the most effective way to pursue the best interests of others as well as our own.

What we need today, and I believe this book will make a valuable contribution to it, is education among individuals and nations, from small children up to political leaders, to inculcate the idea that violence and the demonization of our opponents are counterproductive, that they are not a realistic way to solve our problems. Instead of attributing blame to others, we need to take responsibility ourselves and engage in seeking solutions in a spirit of compassion and humility. Genuine peace and reconciliation, whether in relation to ourselves or in relation to others, comes about through taking an understanding, respectful, and nonviolent approach to our problems.

THE DALAI LAMA (SIGNED)
February 28, 2005

Preface

Conflicts often escalate from relatively minor and tolerable proportions to more and more destructive forms. In this negative spiral, the harsher the conflict, the more we tend to demonize the opponent. We may begin with mere suspicion, surmising that behind the opponent's overt acts, deeper-lying negative intentions lurk. Gradually, inner suspicion turns to blaming, and blaming swells to an accusing certainty. Sometimes, we reach a point where we dismiss any neutral or positive acts on the opponent's part as manipulative. Since these processes tend strongly to mutuality, each party comes to believe he[1] is able to read into the darkest motives of the other and into the destructive forces that control his behavior. Our duty is then to make the opponent own up to his negative intentions, developing the readiness to abjure them. Failing that, we see no alternative but to force him to comply. At this stage, the opponent has been turned into a clear cut enemy. The damages and suffering that are inflicted on him are now seen as inescapable; actually he has brought them upon himself. Also the readiness to inflict pain on third parties or even on our own party grows apace, being viewed as the necessary price in what is increasingly viewed as a battle for survival. Needless to say, demonization blocks compromise solutions, for these would only give the presumed enemy a better chance to pursue his harmful goals. Understanding and countering demonization may thus be the key factors in the prevention and positive management of conflicts.

[1]Masculine and feminine forms are alternated throughout the book.

At times, people also relate with suspicion and hostility toward some putative hidden element within themselves. They may come to believe that a destructive force has become lodged within them, conspiring against their best interests, making them stumble, and working at cross-purposes with their own goals, values, and feelings. They search for ways to expose it, and look for specialists to help in its detection and expulsion. It then seems that this "enemy within" tenaciously evades discovery or fights back to stay in place. Expelling the enemy within will supposedly involve suffering. This effort, however, will be worthwhile, for life will be renewed.

The term *demonization* seems apt to describe both the interpersonal and the intrapersonal varieties of this process; the suspicious and fearful attitude toward the presumed enemy, the attempt to unmask his underlying destructive intentions, the feeling he eludes us, and the wish to expel or destroy him remind us of what fighting with demons is supposed to be like. These features seem to characterize both personal and intimate conflicts as well as group, ethnic, and political ones. As in the religious variety of demonology, the putative fight against demons is conducted both in the most intimate spheres and in the widest social or even cosmic ones.

The demonic view is both an answer to the riddle of suffering and a way of coping with overpowering fear. The mental riddle is solved by the contention that suffering comes from evil. The demonic view thus reflects the refusal to accept that suffering may be the result of chance. Blind accidental suffering is a "cosmic scandal" that the human mind feels bound to reject. Suffering that is caused by an evil force is at least understandable; someone or something has willed it. In addition, such an explanation offers a target. This offers also a solution to the paralysis of fear; fear is mobilized into anger and hatred.

In the Western world, the most influential form of the demonic view has been the belief in Satan. The fight against the satanic powers was viewed as the believer's chief obligation. Any show of indifference, wavering, or doubt was a proof of betrayal. The forces of virtue developed tools that made them capable of tackling the supernatural evil powers. Chief among these were the skills of the inquisitor for the unmasking of witches and heretics, of the exorcist for the expulsion of demons, and of the crusader for the large-scale suppression of the enemies of the faith. The fight against evil, no matter how bitter, was fanned by the highest hopes, for victory would bring salvation. Actually, the harsher the fight, the stronger were the hopes of redemption, and vice versa. Thus, millenarian movements were usually accompanied by outbursts of spontaneous and organized violence against the assumed agents of Satan (Cohn, 1957, 1975; Guinzburg, 1991). The private stage of the traditional demonic narrative was the individual soul, in which a duel was continuously waged between the forces of light and darkness. The believer's chief helper in this fight was not the great inquisitor but the personal confessor, with whose assistance the individual tried to hunt down the dark voices within him. Each person's soul was thus viewed as a microcosm in which the battle for world redemption was waged.

The religious demonic narrative has had many lay parallels. Thus, the structure of some extremist right-wing or left-wing political ideologies can be quite similar to that of traditional demonic views. These ideologies define a segment of society as the conveyor of social redemption (e.g., the master race or the working classes) and another segment as responsible for all ills (e.g., the Jews or the putative forces of social reaction); they develop a lore that is given the status of prophetic truth (e.g., a racial theory or a simplified form of Marxist analysis), an apparatus for finding and hunting down the enemy (e.g., the secret police), and a procedure for cleansing society of its influence (e.g., reform, detention, or extermination camps); they also envisage an apocalyptic war to end all wars and paint an alluring image of the ensuing millennium. In this book, we are concerned chiefly with the intimate lay parallel of traditional demonology. We shall be dealing particularly with demonization at the level of the marriage, the family, and other close personal relationships. We believe, however, that the demonizing processes at these personal, intimate levels are very similar to those that characterize sociopolitical conflicts. Chapter 4 is devoted to spelling out these similarities and their practical consequences for the constructive management of any form of conflict.

Besides analyzing the demonic mindset, we present an alternative to it. In many cultures, an attitude to life, which we shall term *the tragic view*, has militated against the demonic one, providing a completely different answer to the riddle of suffering. The basic assumptions of the tragic view are that suffering is an essential feature of life, that for many kinds of suffering, nobody is to blame and that often the best one can do is to strive for partial amelioration and constructive acceptance. We argue that the tragic view provides an antidote to the demonic view, and that far from engendering hopeless indifference, it inspires compassion and a decided readiness to resist the human propagation of suffering.

In chapter 1, we describe the demonic experience, whereby a common and probably transitory state of suspicion can be aggravated and stabilized by habits of mind that turn it into an accusing certainty and to a demand for the elimination of the putative enemy. Chapter 2 presents the demonic and tragic assumptions in daily life and in psychotherapy: it shows how popular psychology can perpetuate habits of thought that traditionally involved belief in demons and exorcism, and how the tragic view provides an antidote to this mindset. Chapter 3 deals with practical tools for conducting an antidemonic dialogue in psychotherapy and in daily life. Chapter 4 deals with nondemonic fighting both at the personal and the social levels. Nondemonic fighting should enable effective self-defense against violence and oppression, while avoiding escalation and mutual destructiveness. Chapter 5 deals with the neglected role of the tragic virtues of acceptance and consolation in modern life and in psychotherapy.

We did not invent most of the ideas in this book, but merely "modernized" them somewhat. Our sources of inspiration are many. One of us (N. Alon) is indebted to Tibetan Buddhism; the other (H. Omer) is indebted to Gandhi's nonviolent resistance. We were also influenced by many authors within the psychotherapeutic tradition who worked antidemonically without explicitly employing this term. We would like to mention a few of these authors, with the proviso that the list is far from exhaustive. In the narrative or in the solution-oriented tradition, writers such as, Michael White, David Epston (1990), and Steve de Shazer (1985) have presented much positive criticism, as well as creative alternatives, to psychopathological constructions that foster the belief in the hidden "enemy inside." Writers in the cognitive tradition in psychotherapy, especially Aharon T. Beck (Beck, Rush, Shaw, & Emery, 1982), have taught much about how to develop a constructive dialogue that may moderate the black-and-white formulations that are typical of demonic thinking. Systemic thinkers, such as, Gregory Bateson (1972), have helped to develop an antidote against the essentialist mentality that depicts behavior as stemming from hidden agents within the mind, such as demons or pathogens. In the psychoanalytic camp, writers, such as, Heinz Kohut (1971, 1977), and proponents of the intersubjective approach (e.g., Stolorow, Atwood & Brandchaft, 1994), have contributed a crucial corrective to the suspicious attitude of some forms of clinical thinking, allowing for the evolution of an empathetic approach in which even the client's negative characteristics are seen as reflecting legitimate human needs and goals. Another psychoanalyst, James Mann (1973), based his time-limited psychotherapy on the tension between the individual's redemptive strivings and the tragic limitations of his condition. In the field of general psychology, Elizabeth Loftus (Loftus & Ketcham, 1994), Richard Ofshe (1992) and Nicholas Spanos (1996), have helped to debunk the presumptions of what we term the "psycho-demonic view". Stephen Hayes and his associates (Hayes, Strosahl, & Wilson, 1999), whose work we came to know as we were already quite advanced in our own project, developed a therapeutic approach that is very close to what we have termed *the tragic view.* We hope that none of these authors will take offense at our describing them as activists in the antidemonic front.

We would also like to stress that our own work as therapists is neither as successful nor as elegant as most of the examples in this book . In this book, we did not include downright failures, although we surely have plenty of them. We advise the reader to balance the successful examples in the book by using his better judgment. All of the case examples were camouflaged so as to protect the identity of clients. A small number of cases are actually composites of different clients and therapies.[2]

[2]This book is being published simultaneously in English and in Hebrew. Chapters 1 and 3 were translated into English by Shoshana Loudon Sappir. Chapters 2, 4, and 5 were in English in the original.

1

The Demonic Experience

The *demonic view* is a way of experiencing, an evolving attitude that begins with doubt, thrives with suspicion, ends with certainty, and aims at decisive militant action. When it seeps into a relationship, a highly negative view of the other evolves, which in turn may lead to symmetrical counter accusations. Thus a vicious circle arises in which both sides become more and more entrenched in their negative positions.

A few years ago one of us went on a trek to the Himalayas with two friends. The trek was long and difficult and we lost our trail. For 3 days we searched for the trail in vain. One of our friends was injured and we decided to go back. To ease our burden, we buried a large part of our equipment in a hiding place. On our way, we met shepherds and they helped us go back to town. After a few days of recovery, we decided that my friends would stay in town to continue recuperating while I went back to get the equipment we buried. I invited the shepherd, Greeboram, who had helped us find our way to be my guide and porter. I thought that even though he did not speak English, we could communicate—after all, we already had; he had rescued us and we were friends.

My Indian friend, Sani, a mountain climber himself, thought I was making a big mistake:

> You may be doing the right thing and your friend may be a saint. But he knows a lot of money is hidden on your body, and that your equipment is valuable. Even a saint can be tempted. A little shove into an abyss and he'll have enough money for himself and his family for the rest of his life. And who could find you in these wild mountains? Who would look for you?

That thought, which had not entered my mind at all when I agreed with the shepherd to accompany me on the return journey, shook my confidence. My sleep wandered. I was afraid. I imagined a nightmare scenario: Greeboram is walking behind me, the path is lost, mud, fog, a little push, a fall off the cliff. Maybe I was taking a big risk because of naiveté.

I decided to go anyway. Sani did what he could to deter "the potential murderer"; he spoke to Greeboram and explained to him that if we were not back in 5 days a search party would be launched.

We went on our way. In the crowded bus, he was the ideal comrade. He made sure I had a seat. When a woman carrying a child got on, he sat the child on his lap. When an old man got on he moved everybody over to make room for the old man. In the break he helped a passenger who threw up. "False suspicion!" I thought. I was relieved. A potential murderer does not treat people that way. But on the other hand, a potential murderer has to make a friendly impression in order to dupe the intended victim.

At night, Greeboram decided we would not sleep in a hostel. He had relatives where we could sleep and that way we would save money. An isolated hut in the mountains, a few men, food and alcohol. As they drank my hosts got very loud. They urged me to drink. "Maybe they want to get me drunk so it will be easier for them to overcome me," I thought, and politely declined. Now I felt completely alien, alone in a group. Greeboram started getting drunk too. "Alcohol might remove his last inhibitions," I thought, and tried to prevent him from drinking. He responded angrily. At night he decided I would sleep in the only bed in the house, while he would sleep on the doorstep "to guard me." "There!" I thought. A person who did not have malicious intents would not think you needed to guard someone in the home of relatives. I could not sleep. Now there was a conspiracy of murderers against me.

The morning was wonderful. Greeboram and his friends were friendly and breakfast was generous. "What a stupid suspicion," I thought.

We started walking on a narrow and damp path cut into the cliff's edge. Hundreds of meters beneath us the river gushed. Greeboram walked in front of me. There were shreds of ice on the path. Occasionally I faltered. Greeboram would turn around, alarmed, and try to grab me. "Let me walk behind you," he said with hand gestures. "If you slip I can catch you." "Aha!" I thought. "If he walks behind me I will not be able to see when he attacks me."

For 2 days I went back and forth between the two stories— the murderer and the friend. Most of the time I was tense and suspicious and kept a suitable distance. I had to avoid excessive closeness that would make him think I was gullible. I could not enjoy the clumsy conversations with him, because they might have all been deceptive. The hardest thing was that I could not decide which version was true. "When he offers me an apple, is it a gift of generosity or a way to blunt my alertness?" "When he invites his cousin to go with us on the last day, is he doing it as part of the murder plan or only to help the cousin?" The uncertainty was grueling and exhausting.

On the third day, we reached our destination. He carried the heavy equipment. Only then was I relieved. With a load like that you cannot make a serious murder attempt. He had not tried to kill me after all, and I was still there. Greeboram and I parted as friends. Sometimes I wonder whether he picked up any of the doubt and worry I went through with him.

In the demonic mindset, a person looks for hints and signals and scrutinizes the other person for his hidden negative motives. One has to be alert and beware of calm appearances. There is no detail, however small, that cannot become a sign. Seeking for the hidden negative essence, one discards the transient and the innocent as irrelevant. The search for certain truth obviates contradictions and flattens the picture.

The mental attitude that characterizes this process is suspicion, and its inseparable companions are fear and hatred. Once the fear that another intends to harm us enters our hearts, we can no longer be calm. Thinking is impoverished and action rigidified, drying up the positive dialogue between the sides. No stable standing point is left. Many would then prefer the worst certainty to this torture of doubt.

At the beginning of my acquaintance with Greeboram I was grateful and trusted him. I thought, "He wants to help me because he is a good person." That positive view lost its clear hold on my mind when a competing view appeared: "He wants to come with me to kill me and take my money." Each of the two images conformed to the facts; each was in itself reasonable and consequent, but they were not mutually compatible. The negative image spurs the collection of negative evidence, growing more negative in the process. The very existence of doubt may then deepen the threat. In my view of Greeboram, this process did not attain demonic proportions: wavering continued right to the end, and a stable negative view did not prevail. However, the nagging suspicion and the torture of indecision can be a fruitful ground for the development of a full-fledged demonic attitude.

The demonic view is not only something a person keeps to himself. Once doubt and suspicion are cast, trust and openness disappear. Sooner or later the other feels the relationship has become tainted. This may arouse the other's own suspicion, furthering a symmetrical negative process. Things often worsen when one side demands acknowledgment and confession from the other. This demand presents the other with a trap: if she owns up even to a small part of the accusation, she will find out that she has incriminated herself far more than she intended; if she does not, this is viewed as proof of her deviousness. A destructive pattern of "inquisitor and accused" may then come to rule the relationship.

CASE 1

Robert, a friendly and good-tempered 35-year-old designer, remembered one day that when he was 20, he decided to break up with his girlfriend, Silvia, but a month later changed his mind and married her. Now, 15 years later, he began to be plagued by doubts: What did she do in the month they were not together? He asked her and she told him she had been heartbroken, but to ease her suffering had engrossed herself in work and went out with another boy a few times. A terrible suspicion gnawed at him: Did they have sex? The thought was unbearable. Silvia denied it, but Robert did not believe her. He remembered that at the time, she was gloomy and somber. Was it because she had given up the relationship with the other boyfriend? Was it because she missed the good sex she had had with the boyfriend? He did not believe her denials and demanded she swear to them. She swore about the truth of her denials but Robert went on disbelieving her. She had to prove she did not have sex in the month of September, 15 years ago; only conclusive evidence could erase the stain that was cast upon their love. Silvia had been given the impossible task of wiping off the stain and bringing the two of them back to the lost paradise of their relationship before the fateful break.

Silvia tried to be helpful. She reconstructed her movements in the difficult month and showed Robert that she did not have time for an affair. Robert raved: "The fact that you remember so many details after such a long time proves your conscience is not clean." Robert interrogated her in detail, promising that he only needed to have a full picture in order for him to calm down. The more Silvia cooperated, the more he pressed her. She feared that if she stopped answering, things would get even worse. Still, Robert felt she was evasive. Perhaps she was doing this purposely in order to hurt him. Silvia, in turn, suspected that Robert only wanted to torment her, that he did not love her anymore, and might be actually scheming to break up the relationship. "Maybe he has somebody?" Each of the partners was now engaged in uncovering negative motives in the other. Sex became less and less frequent, providing each of them further proof of the other's lack of love. Silvia told the story to a friend, who hypothesized that Robert was acting out of repressed guilt because of his forbidden wishes. "He ought to go to therapy to understand his real motives," the friend concluded. Robert responded to Silvia's suggestion with rage: "You are trying to shun the real issue by blaming *me* for psychological problems! No way!" The deadlock was now complete; both were sure the other was underhandedly motivated, and both looked for ways to catch the other in a revealing slip.

In this case, the demonizing process has grown beyond mere suspicion. The mutual assumption of hidden motives, the dynamics of the inquisitor and the accused, and the redemptive wish that the relationship be returned to its pristine condition are typical to this kind of interaction. Still, some classical demonizing elements are missing in this case. Thus there is still just the germ of what we shall term a *psychodemonic hypothesis*, postulating that the person stands under the control of a hidden power foreign to her consciousness and intentions, which demands uncovering and radical treatment. Such a development is illustrated in the following case.

CASE 2

Rose came to therapy with a strange dilemma. She was in the 6th month of pregnancy and had undergone an experience that convinced her she should by no means become a mother. She wanted to have an abortion, even though at this advanced stage of pregnancy, the abortion actually meant a forced delivery. She believed that only if she succeeded in reliving her early experiences of abuse with her own mother, would she become ripe to be a mother herself. Because of the time pressure, she wanted a very intensive and extremely short treatment. She believed that only deep hypnosis could help her relive her childhood trauma and rid herself of the perverted mother image she carried within herself. Failing this, she insisted on getting rid of the baby.

Rose and her husband had lived abroad until the 3rd month of her pregnancy. There she had participated in a group treatment for future mothers. In this treatment, she became aware that she nurtured narcissistic fantasies about her future daughter that would, in all probability, turn her into a psychologically abusive mother who would exploit her daughter for her own self-aggrandizement. She also found out in the group that she had been psychologically abused by her mother in exactly the same way. The group experience had been powerful, but had not led her to contemplate an abortion. Rose hoped she would overcome her fantasies by confronting her mother and by coping with her own memories of psychological abuse. She continued in individual therapy with the group leader and had a series of lengthy phone conversations with her mother. She wanted to remember what exactly the mother had done to her and wanted the mother to own up to her transgressions. By this confrontation, Rose hoped to become able to vent her repressed anger and get rid of the internalized image of her mother in her unconscious. This would allow her to become the free person she might have always been, making her also ready to be a mother herself. Rose remembered how the mother had made stringent demands on her that she be an outstanding student. She was extremely critical whenever Rose failed, and beamed when she received a prize at school. Rose's feeling, however, was that the mother needed Rose's achievements for herself, to fill in the emptiness inside her. She never cared whether her demands fitted Rose's needs or not, at times riding roughshod over her feelings. Rose remembered hating her ballet school, and yet the mother kept her there for 3 years against her will. The mother would also force Rose to dance before whomever came into the house, to show off Rose's accomplishments. Rose remembered how unwilling and humiliated she felt, and how the mother smiled and her face got red with pleasure at Rose's expense. To Rose's consternation and anger, the mother denied that it had been so. She had never forced Rose to anything at all. The mother's tone in the phone was self-justifying and apologetic; she had meant well and she believed Rose would be thankful afterward. At times, the mother would burst out crying, failing to understand what had made Rose hate her so much. In one of the conversations, the mother changed her tone, and instead of justifying herself, started yelling back at Rose. Suddenly, Rose had a feeling of cringing physically in fear of her mother's voice. She talked to her therapist (the group leader) about this feeling, and the therapist commented that probably the mother had used more than mere moral pressure to get Rose to comply. Rose feared confronting the mother with this possibility. When she came back to Israel (now on her 6th month of pregnancy), she decided to get to the root of this experience, and only then bring the mother face-to-face with the truth.

Rose's new therapist was in a quandary. He knew that a hypnotic attempt to relive the childhood trauma might bring up pseudomemories of things that had never happened. The recent history of psychotherapy is full with such examples, which often end in families breaking up, the patient's condition deteriorating and, sometimes, with the therapist being sued by the patient for having led her to believe in false memories. The therapist explained this to Rose and presented her with the evidence about the unreliability of hypnosis in the recovery of repressed memories. Rose was shocked. She asked the therapist what could be done. The therapist proposed to have a series of sessions to discuss Rose's pregnancy, her feelings about impending motherhood, and her relationship with her mother. Luckily, Rose agreed, and the therapist felt he had bought time.

The therapist saw Rose for about 2 months. He told her that she was in a position to avoid making the same mistakes her mother perhaps had made. They talked about Rose's fantasies about the baby. She had dreamt, to her horror, that the baby would become a famous ballet dancer! In another dream, she was attending her own funeral, but when the coffin was opened, there was a baby lying inside it. This dream had been interpreted by her former therapist as a repetition of Rose's relationship with her own mother; the mother had kept herself mentally alive at the price of her daughter's life. The new therapist consoled Rose that such fantasies, both positive and negative, were common in pregnancy. By no means did they mean that she would force her wishes on her daughter, or rob the daughter of her vitality to serve her own needs. He promised Rose to help her if, in the future, she felt she was in danger of so doing. Rose smiled in relief. Actually, she said, she did not believe she would be like her mother at all. The therapist did not feel strong enough at this stage to challenge Rose's view of her own mother. This was perhaps a mistake, for Rose's relationship with her mother quickly deteriorated. Rose's mother knew most of Rose's old friends because they used to visit their house before Rose's trip abroad. She approached some of these friends, asking for their help in improving her relationship with Rose. Rose reacted furiously, interpreting the mother's action as proof of her manipulative character. She cut off all communications with all of her previous friends. She then moved with her husband to another town without letting the mother know where she was living. She would phone the mother once a month, usually for very short conversations peppered with biting remarks. Rose had no intention of letting her mother see her future granddaughter for quite a long time. The therapy sessions came to an end under this inauspicious star.

Rose's story illustrates how a series of mental and interpersonal elements, which perhaps might not be seen as necessarily belonging together, cluster and conglomerate, creating a coherent set of attitudes that lead to highly repetitive interactions. Some of these elements are already familiar to us from the previous case: a suspicious and blaming attitude, the dynamics of the inquisitor and the accused, the attribution of ulterior motives, and the hope of reattaining a condition of purity by ridding oneself of the negative memories. Some elements are new to this case: a theory of trauma explaining how unconscious "implants" are created (the mother's psychological abuse of Rose), a professional who is able to detect and interpret the hidden signs of trauma (the group therapist), a therapeutic procedure to bring the hidden elements to consciousness and expel them (deep hypnosis), and a growing belief in conspiracies (e.g., between the mother and Rose's friends). We argue that these elements form a whole and fit together as in a puzzle because they follow a cultural blueprint that has been hallowed throughout the ages. This blueprint provides us with a ready-made mental mould with high appeal. The traditional form of this cultural prototype includes the belief in an evil principle (Satan) and its agents (demons, witches, heretics); the conviction that these powers camouflage themselves as best they can so as to escape detection and gain control; the belief in a science (demonology) that is able to unmask them, and in a set of procedures for hunting them down (inquisition) and expelling them (exorcism). What we term the *psychodemonic view* is the psychological lay counterpart of this traditional blueprint.

Perhaps, however, the high cohesiveness of this cultural prototype might, under favorable conditions, help bring about its dissolution; if it were possible to insert, as it were, an "antidemonic solvent" into the demonic conglomerate, one might hope that it would gradually fall apart. Hostile suspicion is probably the chief emotion and motive in the demonizing process. The opposite of hostile suspicion is empathy and compassion. When we empathize with the other and compassionately participate in his suffering (com = with, passion = suffering), mutual alienation and hostility diminish. The following case illustrates such a surprising dissolution.

CASE 3

Leon and Margaret, who had been in therapy a few times in the past, sought help again because of a difficult family situation. Their youngest son, Danny, had decided not to join the family business run by the father and chose to go to Nepal as part of a group of mountain climbers. The son informed his father he did not see himself as a factory man in the future either. When his father asked him what plans he had for the future, the son said curtly that he would continue climbing mountains until he decided what to do with his life.

Leon, who was born in Greece, and who was a working man since his youth, was shattered. Danny's refusal to join the family business was a terrible blow for Leon. He felt as if his life's work and dream, the Aroesti and Sons Company, had been destroyed. Leon's anger grew as he explained his position to the therapist: "Danny doesn't give a damn about the family and the future. He laughs at me and cares only for himself. He knows I need him but he couldn't care less. He will sacrifice the family business just to have a good time. If he doesn't come back, I don't know what I'll do. He won't be my son anymore." Margaret wept throughout the session. "Leon, he's your son. What kind of way is that to talk about him? Do you really think he doesn't care about us? Let him develop the way he feels." Leon burst out: "Are you defending him again? You never support me. You and the boys! You always defended them. You never took my side. Who have I worked for all these years? Can't you see that this business is not just mine? It is all of ours!"

Everyone tried to explain to Leon that his son was doing what was normal these days, that young people have to find their own way, that working in a family business is a hard choice for a young person, and that he should not pressure his son. The therapist did this too. It worked like oil on fire: "Why do I have to understand him and not him me? How long do I have to understand him? At his age, I was married and was deep in the business. We ruined our kids because we gave them everything without demanding anything in return. Mountain climbing! And you all encourage him!"

Unlike Danny, Joe, the oldest son, worked as a production manager in the factory. There was constant tension between the father and the son because Joe's tougher management style did not suit Leon's intense need to maintain a relaxed atmosphere in the factory at all times. When the family moved from Greece to Israel, Leon's father had opened a small workshop. As Leon grew up and started a family of his own, his father handed the management of the factory over to him and his father had stayed on in a junior position. However, his father endlessly criticized Leon's management methods. Leon oscillated between furious silences and enraged outbursts. He swore he would act differently and pass the firm's managements to his sons in time. However, Danny's "betrayal" threatened Leon's dream of retiring from the active management of the factory by handing it over to Joe and Danny. Margaret thought that Leon's critical attitude toward his sons was a perfect a replica of his father's attitude toward him. She also believed that Leon was punishing her for daring to think differently than him. The rift thus threatened to swallow her as well.

The therapist was overcome with frustration. He felt that Margaret was seeing the situation for what it was and that Leon was in total denial of the truth. For the first time in their joint life and in the year-long history of intermittent but helpful therapeutic encounters, the therapist was stymied and Margaret could not help him reach Leon in his anger. The soft, gentle man who would not hurt a fly had become a demanding tyrant. The therapist began to think that in this case, unconscious negative forces might well be at work. However, his attempts to help Leon become aware of the deepset irrational nature of his reactions made him become even more entrenched. Leon now felt misunderstood and betrayed by all, even by the therapist. The therapist tried meeting with him individually in the hope of somehow getting across to him. Leon, however, wanted solidarity with his views and not psychological interpretations. He now felt cornered by a conspiracy involving the children, Margaret, and the therapist.

Just at that time the therapist was invited to give a workshop in Greece about resolving tensions in the family. To prepare, he read a book about family life in Greece. Reading the book led him to view Leon in a new light. He phoned Leon from abroad and said: "I have just read a book about Greece that changed my whole outlook on you and the situation. I realized that I badly misunderstood you. When I come back I want to talk to you about it because I feel it will allow us to act in a better way." Leon was very curious but had to contain his curiosity.

The therapist told the family what he had learned from the book. In Greece, there have been deep changes in family life because of the move of large populations from the village to the city. In the village, the family's grandparents, parents, and children used to live together as a clan in the same house. The clan shared the farm and the whole family worked on it. The idea that a member of the family could leave the homestead and seek independence was inconceivable. The sons worked on the farm and the family head made all the decisions on behalf of the clan. He was the farming expert, the judge, and the guide. When a young man grew up and came of age, the family married him off. Upon his marriage, the oldest son became heir to the throne, an upcoming leader training to become head of the family. Gradually the father would relinquish his authority and relegate to his son, and thus retreat to the position of "wise advisor". That was the order of things in Greek society, and it worked for countless generations.

Leon listened carefully. Although he had not grown up in Greece, he apparently knew what the therapist was talking about. The process of modernization in Greece changed all that. Countless families migrated to the cities. The joint homestead was sold and the clan split up. Education and a trade promised young people a better future in the modern world. Countless crises erupted. The parents thought that if they had to go to the city, they would do so together. If they built a new business, it would be a family business. When children opted out of the family business, the parents felt the children were giving up the only source of security the family had ever known. Such an act was not only irresponsible—it was also a betrayal that weakened the whole family. The sons, in turn, viewed their fathers' demand that they live and work with the large family on the homestead or elsewhere as tyrannous.

Therapist: Leon, I believe that your family operated in this tradition. When I read those descriptions I understood that your wish to resign from the business and give the leadership to your children was not an arbitrary wish to tie them down as they—and I admit, I too—thought. The deep motive of all of your actions was not a tyrannical wish, or the result of a psychological problem, but your concern for your family and the desire to keep it together. Perhaps, when I gave you a psychological interpretation, I even made it more difficult for Margaret to understand this. I believe this misunderstanding is the source of much of the mutual anger.

Leon: Now you are making sense! That is exactly how I feel! I tried to explain it a thousand times but nobody understood. What is so hard to understand here? And why are you all so angry with me all the time?

Therapist: What is happening to you is what is happening to many families. The good old values cannot work smoothly anymore. The world in which you grew up is no longer understandable to your sons, and you do not understand the world in which they grew up. The rift is very painful, but inevitable. It is not Danny or you who are responsible, but something that happens to both of you. Probably neither you nor he could have reacted differently. Danny is a son of the present generation, just like you, Margaret, and I are children of the previous generation. You cannot accept his values, but neither can he accept yours. If Margaret could not understand your crisis, if I, your therapist, could not understand it, how can you expect the 22-year-old Danny to understand it?

Leon: Actually, where did I get that outlook? After all, I grew up in Israel. I was not part of my parents' world. We hardly talked to each other. I grew up on the streets.

Margaret: You were not raised by your mother and father. They were too busy in the early years.

Leon: That's right! I was raised by my grandmother! And that is exactly how she viewed the family!

Margaret: Leon, Danny is a good boy. He cares about us. It is true he does not tell us things, it is true he has different interests, but the family matters to him. He is very unhappy about the rift between you.

Leon: But I want to give him everything. I want him to run the business with Joe. He will not find such an opportunity anywhere!

Therapist: The book I read shows the anguish of fathers who went through exactly what you are going through. But I am sure Danny is not betraying you. If he hears the Greek story, he will certainly understand you. Speak to him. I will be glad to talk to him on the phone and tell him what I think. Don't let the relationship between you break off. Stay in touch with him. As for Joe, let him run things his way. Even if there are bumps on the way, in the end he will succeed. And one day you will be able to go on the long trip abroad you are dreaming of, knowing the business is running well without you.

Leon's anger dissipated. He and Margaret spoke to Danny. They explained the Greek story to him. Danny continued climbing mountains for a while, and then got into the university. A follow-up communication a few years later showed the family did not return to a pattern of blame and counterblame.

Leon remembers the Greek story as a turning point in his life and the life of his family. He likes the fact that he belongs to an ancient tradition, yet he is aware of the difficulties that stem from the inevitable friction between it and modern reality. He is proud of his Greekness and intends to study his community of origin in depth.

The reader may rightfully wonder how a tough cloud of mutual suspicion that hung over the family for long dissipated in one session. Can that be? Indeed, that resolution surprised the therapist no less than the family. The impact of the therapist's empathic intervention in this case was probably facilitated by many factors: the therapist's standing with the couple, the family's strong emotional bonds, and perhaps, the fact that Leon, Margaret, and Danny were already waiting for a chance to stop fighting anyway. The therapist's empathic and compassionate message probably provided a catalyst to the other positive factors. The intervention was not only empathic, but involved an additional factor: It redescribed the clash between Leon and Danny as the tragic result of inexorable historical and cultural processes. Leon and Danny were exonerated of bad intentions, personal defects, or psychological distortions. Both had acted humanly and understandably under the circumstances. The negative aspects that emerged were not willed, but were the by-products of fate. Such a tragic redescription is, as we argue, the best antidote to the demonic view.

Chapter **2**

The Demonic and the Tragic Views[1]

Throughout the ages, people's ideas about human nature were mainly influenced by religion. Our beliefs about the condition of the soul and the causes of suffering and happiness were mostly a function of the current religious creeds. For most of the population, lay ideas and ideologies had only a marginal influence on these themes. The situation has changed radically in the course of the last two centuries. Today, for most people in the Western world, the influence of religion has receded drastically, giving way to a variety of lay social and psychological views on human nature and goals. Popular versions of the prevailing psychological theories have attained a vast influence over all areas of life. Popular psychology has also penetrated into the way people talk with each other in intimate contact or to themselves in their secluded moments. "Psychologese" is a common language in the family, at school, and at times, even in business and politics. And yet, in spite of the depth of this transformation, we shall argue that some of the themes and habits of thought that characterized religious discourse also pervaded modern psychology, especially in the forms that are most appealing to the general public. In particular what we shall term the *demonic view* of human nature greatly influences psychological thinking and practice and determines much of the impact of this thinking on the public. We believe that the psychological version of the demonic view allows psychotherapists and consumers of popular psychology to

[1]This chapter is an expanded version of: Alon, N. & Omer, H. (2004). Demonic and tragic narratives in psychotherapy. In Lieblich, A., McAdams, D. P., & Josselson, R. (Eds.), *Healing plots: The narrative basis of psychotherapy* (pp. 29–48). Washington, DC: APA Press.

engage in thought patterns that in the past involved the belief in witches, Satan, and demonic possession. In this chapter, we describe the psychodemonic view that we regard as the psychological counterpart of the religious variety of demonic thinking. We shall also describe an alternative view on human nature, which we shall term the *tragic view*. The two views deal with the problem of suffering: The demonic view postulates that suffering comes from evil qualities or intentions. Evil can be manifested as abuse, neglect, perversion, greed, or various forms of harmful conspiracy. "Tragic" is opposed to "demonic" in the assumption that suffering is inseparable from life. Suffering does not require an explanation in terms of an external specific cause. Suffering is but the feeling side of human fallibility, vulnerability, and mortality.

In its radical form, the demonic view is usually rather marginal both in the religious and the psychological establishments. However, particularly under conditions of acute social or cultural upheaval, it may spread quickly to the general population, where it often undergoes further simplification and radicalization. Society may then be swept by epidemics of "pop religion" or, modernly, pop psychology, where possession and exorcism (both in their religious and psychological guise) become almost daily phenomena. In religious history, these popular epidemics have often reflected back onto the establishment; the official church then adopted views that were once the preserve of marginal groups. The same often happens in psychology; the crude psychodemonic views to be described are usually not characteristic of the mainstream of professional thinking. However, with the appropriate media coverage, fringe ideas may spread quickly and reflect back on clinical practice. The epidemic of multiple-personality disorder and the belief in the spread of satanic cults in the 1980s cannot be understood without this backlash influence of pop psychology over psychology.

Although we cannot, in the confines of this book, do justice to the cultural richness of the demonic and the tragic views, we would like to mention some of their historical manifestations. The *demonic view* consists of the belief that evil forces are responsible for human suffering, and that an all-out fight against them is the only way to save humankind. Victory over the forces of evil signifies far more than a local victory over suffering; it restores the lost innocence of society and the individual, thus leading to salvation. The demonic view involves the belief in total innocence and purity. The fight against evil actually aims at the recovery of the lost paradise. Some well-known historic examples of this split are that between God and Satan in Christianity, the battle between light and darkness in the Zoroastrian religion, and the polarity of spirit and matter in neoplatonic and gnostic philosophies. There are also fully secular versions of the demonic view, such as the Nazi split between pure and impure races, the Marxist division of the world into exploiters and the exploited, and the cold war mentality of total suspicion.

The *tragic view* reflects the understanding that redemptive hopes are invariably illusory. Facts of life such as aging, illness, bereavement, and death cannot be denied, eliminated, or wished away. Also social suffering, far from being the result of an evil conspiracy, is usually the outcome of an interplay between desires and goals, all of which may be basically legitimate. One of the sources for the tragic view is Buddhism, with its view of suffering as often evolving out of people's attempt to realize their positive life wishes. Buddhism is also antidemonic in its rejection of a dualistic view of good and evil. The tragic view has also a long tradition in Western culture, for instance, in Greek and Elizabethan tragedy, as well as in the work of philosophers, such as, Epicurus, Epictetus, Marcus Aurelius, Montaigne, Spinoza, and Schopenhauer. Our chief contemporary source for the tragic view is the French thinker André Compte-Sponville (1984), whose *Treatise of Despair and Beatitude* can be viewed as a modern primer on the tragic view and spiritual serenity.

THE PSYCODEMONIC VIEW

Demonic thinking, whether in its traditional or psychological guise, is characterized by a polarizing logic, as well as by a number of specific assumptions about human nature and the origins of suffering. It is an "either–or" mode of thinking in which everything that exists must be categorized as light or dark, good or bad, us or them, friend or foe. Many sidedness and complexity are viewed as the signs of a weak mind.

Demonic Assumptions

1. All suffering comes from evil. This is the basic demonic postulate; it reflects the refusal to accept that suffering may be the result of chance. In all cultures and ages, people have tried to depict human pain as stemming from a metaphysical evil principle. Since psychologists reject *evil* as an explanatory concept, the psychological counterpart to this demonic assumption takes on a special form; suffering is viewed as stemming from trauma, which leads to the evolution of pathological structures, destructive drives, and negative feelings. Traumatizing parents and other abusers are thus the modern counterparts of the evil principles of yore. If, for instance, my suffering is of the order of x, it must be the case that an x amount of traumatization underlies it. It is only when we succeed in unearthing the usually hidden traumatization that the suffering can be said to have been understood. We might call this assumption *the law of conservation of evil*, on account of its structural similarity to the physical laws of conservation of matter and of energy. This parallel helps to understand the appeal of this assumption. In a problem in physics or chemistry, we say that we have solved the equation once we have shown that the matter or energy at the end is the same as at beginning. Similarly, in the human sphere, we feel that suffering has been explained once we have identified a matching quantum of trauma that underlies it. The mind comes to rest when it succeeds in establishing that what is present at the end was already present at the beginning. This assumption has a compelling quality: Suffering must be due to a proportionate traumatization. If one asks why the person thinks so, one may get a surprised response: "How could it be otherwise?" This self-evident nature underlies the elusiveness and tenacity of this demonic assumption.

The law of conservation of evil implies that the more serious a child's mental condition, the harder the neglect, deprivation, or traumatization the child must have suffered from others. This equation has yielded a whole range of parental evils, corresponding to the gravity of mental disorders. Thus a child who suffers from a relatively circumscribed mental problem, say, an anxiety disorder, will be assumed to have been exposed by her parents to rather localized traumatic experiences (e.g., the parents may have failed to provide the child with a feeling of security, or alternatively may have been overprotective). A child with a more pronounced problem, for instance, one who behaves violently at home and at school, would necessarily be assumed to have been neglected and/or battered by his parents. If, in addition, the violence becomes manifest in the sexual sphere, and the child grows up to become a sexual molester, this is tantamount to proof that the child was sexually molested by the parents or by another party. The worst kind of parental mismanagement would be attributed to the parents of children with the worst mental disorders. Thus, schizophrenic children were supposed to have "schizophrenogenic" mothers; this is a special kind of "monster" whose extreme destructiveness is only matched by its equally extreme deviousness (e.g., Bateson, Jackson, Haley, & Weakland, 1956; Fromm-Reichman, 1948). Such a mother continuously attacks the child while declaring her unconditional motherly love. These links between child disorder and parenting are not usually corroborated by empirical data. The link is rather "It must be so!" With such an underlying assumption, even the flimsiest piece of evidence may be accepted as incontrovertible proof.

2. The presumed enemy is an evil and dissembling creature. Demonization means regarding other persons as demons, that is, as unnatural and evil creatures that constantly conspire to destroy you. The absolute "otherness" of the presumed enemy is clearest when whole groups are demonized. Jews, witches, and lepers, for instance, were often viewed as absolute aliens who poisoned the wells of the faithful to take revenge for their own deformity. In personal relations, demonization evolves when the feeling takes hold that the intimate other is, in some negative way, essentially different from oneself. At these moments, empathy breaks down, giving way to suspicion and aversion. The most puzzling form of this attribution of otherness occurs in self-demonization; the individual then becomes convinced that some hostile power has infiltrated her very self and is conspiring against her. Self-demonization is closely linked to demonization of others, for the inner hostile factor is actually a representative of an external destructive power. Thus in the religious variety of demonization, the inner enemy is an agent of Satan; in the psychological variety of demonization, the inner enemy is an introject of the abusing parent or a dissociated element of the repressed traumatic experience. The infiltration of the self is thus invariably the result of an external attack.

In situations of interpersonal conflict, people tend to view their antagonists as essentially different from themselves. In a fight, one experiences one's own pain, one's own need for self-protection, and the justness of one's own cause, but not the pain of the other party, its right for self-protection, or the justness of its cause. The more acute the conflict, the more one tends to polarize the world into "us" and "them." The antagonists are then viewed as though they were made of a different stuff altogether.

A process similar to that of interpersonal conflict might explain how one learns to view the party within the self that seems to work at cross-purposes to one's goals as an alien. The reasoning might work as follows:

1. We often cause ourselves damage.
2. We do not feel any desire to cause this damage.
3. The damaging acts must therefore be caused by an alien and hostile element within us.

This inner alien is not part of the "I", but rather an "it." Accordingly, Freud termed the substrate of blind drives within the mind the *id* (Latin for "it"). In contemporary discourse, the "it" has multiplied itself into a veritable population explosion of inner aliens: early traumas, dissociated experiences, hidden personalities, repressed drives, automatisms, unreleased energies, implanted programs (e.g., by cults), subliminal suggestions, propaganda residues, and whatnot. No wonder our behavior sometimes seems to us more like a frenzied Stravinsky choreography than an organic process.

Psychological discourse has given the inner alien an aura of scientific respectability. The professional terms that describe it seem to obviate any links with popular superstition. Nothing would seem farther from demons or possession than concepts like *multiple personality disorder, dissociated ego-state*, or *hysterical fugue.* Consider, however, the following two quotes:

> Our parents plant mental and emotional seeds in us—seeds that grow as we do ... As you grew into adulthood, these seeds grew into invisible weeds that invaded your life in ways you never dreamed of. Their tendrils may have harmed your relationships, your career, or your family; they have certainly undermined your self-confidence and self esteem. (Forward, 1990, p. 5)

> The problem many trauma victims face is that the upsetting experience from the past ... is "stuck" in their nervous system. Like a puppet-master, this old experience governs the person's reactions to present-day situations. (Shapiro & Forrest, 1997, p.23)

These descriptions cannot be said to be true or false in a scientific sense. One could hardly conceive of a scientific experiment that could refute them. Rather than contentions about fact, they are ways of depicting reality that reflect the writers' preferences. In other words, they are culturally conditioned narratives. The point we are trying to make is that these narratives are highly similar to traditional demonic ones; by changing only a few words, one could easily insert these quotes into the *Malleus Maleficarum*, the standard text about witches and demons from the late Middle Ages.

3. Innocence is the basic human condition. The Biblical story of Adam's fall embodies this assumption in its prototypical form. Humankind was originally innocent and blissful, but through the influence of the snake, it lost the Garden of Eden and its pristine purity. What is called original sin thus reflects a state of decay relative to the basic condition of original innocence. Redemption consists in the restoration of the lost state of purity and bliss. This, however, can only be achieved by purging the evil that has entered the soul.

The assumption of original innocence is manifest also in lay versions. Thus in many utopias, the ideal society of the future is described as a return of the lost golden age. The communist millennium, for instance, is often depicted as an industrialized version of primeval communism, the Romantic's paradise as a return to the natural state of the innocent savage, and the nationalist's dream as a return to tribal roots. Abrams (1971) coined the expression *natural supernaturalism*, to designate the idealized spiritual biography of the Romantic that follows almost fixedly through the stations of original bliss, fall, conversion, self-purging, and salvation. As in the religious cosmic cycle, the end coincides with the beginning and the millennium is paradise regained. The pilgrimage is actually circular: "Where are we going? Always home!" says the German poet Novalis (Abrams, 1971, p. 390). In psychology, varieties of this romantic life cycle are at times very popular. For instance, the child is often viewed as essentially innocent and good, a condition that is only lost because of the parents' crass misunderstanding or neglect of the child's needs. The adult, however, can become whole again by recontacting the forgotten child within her. Thus, Miller (1981), the author of *The Drama of the Gifted Child* (1981), claimed that all human destructiveness results from the warping of the child's original innocence by parental abuse. This abuse constitutes a deep hidden secret that, once revealed, must lead to personal and social redemption:

> I was amazed to discover that I had been an abused child, that from the very beginning of my life I had no choice but to comply totally with the needs and feelings of my mother and ignore my own ... It was thanks to the pain of the child in me that I fully grasped what so many adults must ward off all their life, and I also realized why they fail to confront their truth, *preferring instead to plan self-destruction on a gigantic atomic scale,* without even recognizing the absurdity of what they are doing. These are the same people who, like all of us, *entered the world as innocent infants, with the primary goals of growing, living in peace, and loving—never of destroying life* ... I recognized the compelling logic of this absurdity after I found the missing piece of the puzzle: the secret of childhood, till then closely guarded. (pp. xii-xv, emphasis added).

This assumption of an original innocence that is shattered by a faulty upbringing has become one of the mainstays of popular and of not-so-popular psychology. In its popular guise, the belief comes across in current sayings, such as "There are no bad children, but only children who are badly treated"; in its professional guise, the belief is illustrated by the reaction of a psychologist to a lecture on violence against siblings given by one of the authors (H. Omer): "You forgot to mention that such violence inevitably results from a destruction of the child's basic attitude of trust!"

The attractiveness of the "innocence" assumption is understandable. It leaves room for hope, for what was lost can perhaps be regained. Historically, it has also played a positive role, helping in the fight against the maltreatment of children. However, when belief in the innocence of the child is bought at the price of the demonization of parents, the assumption may cause considerable harm.

4. The roots of evil lie hidden. The demonic view posits that only things that "lie deep" are fully real, whereas those that "lie at the surface" are mere symptoms, signifying little. External acts are thus only the outer layer; what matters are the destructive forces underneath. These forces often lie hidden even from their "host." This assumption implies that the mind is composed of insulated compartments, with only the less important and less "real" accessible to consciousness. The devil exploits the compartmentalized nature of the soul to embed itself in its hidden strata, thus taking control of the individual. This view of the soul is essential for both the traditional and the psychological versions of the demonic view.

Psychoanalysis has taught us to equate "deep" with "unconscious." Thus, whatever lies closer to awareness is perforce "superficial" and is therefore less weighty, true, or valid. Acts and thoughts are in this sense more superficial than feelings, conscious feelings more than preconscious ones, and preconscious feelings more than unconscious ones. Real influence is exerted from the bottom upward; the unconscious mind determines what happens in the preconscious and the conscious mind, never the contrary. Any attempt to change one's acts without dealing with the deep feelings underneath would thus be viewed as a mechanical dabbling in externals. Similarly, attending to one's conscious thoughts, examining their validity, or trying to better adapt them to reality is often viewed as a futile intellectual exercise. In daily life, this assumption manifests itself in the common use of the word "real." What somebody "really" feels, "really" wants, or "really" is, is assumed to be quite different from whatever this person consciously feels, wants, or thinks he or she is. We might characterize this attitude as one of pervasive suspicion; it is not possible for the "real" person voluntarily or consciously to reveal herself; the "real" person can only betray herself unwittingly.

5. Detection of the hidden forces requires an esoteric knowledge. The attitude of pervasive suspicion that is characteristic of the demonic view can become manifest at the individual, social, or even metaphysical level. At the individual level, for instance, suspicion manifests itself in the search for the insidious ways in which dark drives and repressed memories control people's lives; at the social level, in tracing the hidden plots of negative groups to take control of society, and at a metaphysical level in the endeavor to unmask the evil powers that are in league to conquer the world. In order to detect this scheming one must learn to interpret its veiled signs and unwitting disclosures. Some people are held to have a special knowledge or acuity for seeing through the superficial positive appearance to the hidden reality underneath: in the past these were the demon doctors (inquisitors and exorcists), who were believed to be versed in the signs that reveal the presence of witches, heretics, and demons. In the present, these are mostly the psychologists and the psychiatrists. For those who do not possess the required knowledge, lists of symptoms that disclose the presence of evil forces or of dangerous psychological phenomena have been made available by the "specialists." Such lists were circulated by the inquisition among the general population at the time of the great witch hunts (Ginzburg, 1991; Ginzburg, A. Tedeschi, & J. Tedeschi, 1992). Similarly, lists of psychological symptoms that presumably indicate, for instance, whether a person was sexually abused as a child, have, at times, become widely accepted both among therapists and among the psychologically minded public (e.g., Blume, 1990). On the Internet, questionnaires that allow one to check whether one suffers from multiple personality or from other fashionable conditions can easily be found. As with most psychological epidemics, the result of these self-exams often turn out to be positive.

Psychologists are popularly viewed as the specialists of the unconscious, from whom nothing can be hidden. With the help of their special tools, psychologists are believed to have access to mental content that is unknown to the client. In case of a discrepancy between the client's judgment and that of the psychologist, the latter is assumed to be preferable. The intuitive sign reader, who interprets the true meaning of the acts of a spouse, child, parent, boss, or employee is thus inspired by a hallowed cultural model. Furthermore she is following the popular psychological more, according to which a critical attitude toward the presumed good intentions of others and self is the hallmark of an insightful person.

The reader may take exception at the parallel drawn between the psychologist's diagnostic tools and the inquisitorial instruments for the detection of witches and demons. Psychologists, after all, do not torture people. An intriguing similarity, however, can be discerned in the attitude of pervasive suspicion. Thus both the psychodiagnostician and the soul doctor focus on the hidden rather than on the manifest, both prize most highly revelations that escape the examinee's conscious guard, both believe that their diagnostic tools are fool-proof, and both turn these tools into a central element of their respective professional identities. Moreover, both resent any skepticism pertaining to their privileged access to the hidden recesses of the soul.

One of the puzzling phenomena in the relationship of many psychologists to psychodiagnostic tools is their consistent preference for those that are rather esoteric, that is, those that putatively reveal the most hidden contents of the soul and that only highly trained clinicians are capable and authorized to use. Despite their relatively low level of objective validation, these are the tools that are most used and trusted by clinical psychologists (Watkins, Campbell, Nieberding, & Hallmark, 1995). These are also the tools that clinical psychologists guard most jealously within their own restricted professional preserve. Chief among these tools are the projective tests (e.g., the Rorschach test, the Thematic Apperction Test and the Draw-a-Person Test) that allegedly enable the diagnostician to read into the deepest secrets of the unconscious. This decided preference for projective tests stands in sharp contrast to the innumerable critical studies that have shown them to be far less valid and useful than more straightforward assessment instruments, such as direct clinical questionnaires and performance tests (e.g., Anastasi, 1982; L. J. Chapman & J. P. Chapman, 1967; Dawes, 1994; Jensen, 1965; Sundberg,

1977; Wood, Nezwozki, Lilienfeld, & Garb, 2003). Straightforward tools, however, consistently fail to find favor with clinicians. Thus, in most training programs in clinical psychology, the greatest attention is devoted to projective tests, whereas very little time is devoted to straightforward questionnaires. These programs tend to gloss over the many studies that show projective tests to be of very questionable validity. Interestingly, the psychologists who conducted these critical studies have become rather unpopular among their colleagues. This negative view of the critics is derived not from the presence of solid contradictory evidence, but rather from the perception of the critics as traitorous.

6. Acknowledgment and confession are the preconditions of cure. In the traditional demonic view, confession lies at the center of the purification process. The skills of the traditional soul doctor that are instrumental in restoring the sinner or the possessed to her right mind are a balanced mixture of benign fatherliness and a threatening inquisitorial stance. In the religious demonic view, there is a fundamental difference between the confessed and the unconfessed sinner; the former can be saved, whereas the latter can only be destroyed. Mere outward confession, however, does not suffice. In order for it to be effective, confession must come from the heart.

In the psychological sphere, what is meant by *the achievement of insight* may be rather similar to a religious confession. It commonly consists in the avowal of one's previously denied negative feelings. It is through this avowal that the person supposedly becomes ripe for a cure. The attempts of spouses, parents and psychotherapists to convince the significant other (spouse, child, or client) to acknowledge her negative feelings and attitudes are often guided by the belief that the other is not only negatively motivated but also, consciously or unconsciously, bent on denying her motives. Only if this denial is overcome is there real hope for change. Confession and insight can of course be of profound spiritual and personal significance; however, when they are driven by a psychodemonic stance, they can become persecutory.

For the person who is yet unaware of her negative feelings and intentions, a period of inquiry and self-examination must precede the confession or achievement of insight. Awareness can either be achieved suddenly or gradually. Thus, in a religious examination, the demon may manifest himself suddenly, to the host's shocking surprise. Often, however, the host becomes gradually aware of how the demon is taking advantage of a person's vulnerable spots to settle himself in the inner recesses of the person. By this growing understanding, the host becomes ripe for confession. She may then acknowledge that she had facilitated the demon's penetration by having lived sinfully. In the psychological process the sequence is often similar; the helper confronts the client with signs in her behavior that indicate the presence of repressed mental material. This previously unrecognized side of the personality sometimes emerges in a sudden revelation, for instance, under hypnosis or in a stormy therapeutic experience. At other times the manifestation is more gradual. In both cases, a process is started whereby the client may become aware of previous occasions when the unacknowledged mental material was present to the mind.

The sometimes nebulous frontiers between the religious process of "becoming ripe for confession" and the psychological one of "attaining insight" were totally effaced in a famous and controversial court case. Paul Ingram was a respected member of his community. He had two daughters and two sons and was a very religious man. In the course of a therapeutic group experience sponsored by the church, his daughter Erika was flooded by vivid images of sexual abuse by her father and many other men within the context of a satanic cult. She also had recollections of other girls who were abused, and babies that were born and sacrificed. In one occasion, she was even forced to eat of the flesh of her murdered baby. A few months after her discovery, her sister Julia also brought to mind a series of events of ritual abuse by their father. The sisters lodged a complaint with the police and the father was immediately arrested. Soon after his incarceration, his pastor together with a psychologist reasoned with him that it was not likely that his daughters, whom he had brought up as believing Christians, were brazenly lying. It was likelier that he was blinded by "satanic deception," which prevented him from remembering his own sins. Ingram was encouraged to pray and ask God to send him revelations about his hidden acts. Any inklings about what he had done were bound to be true, for God would not give him a stone when Ingram asked Him for bread. Ingram was taught a relaxation procedure and was encouraged to let the memories come flooding back. He showed himself a susceptible subject for this kind of mental exercise, and on the very next day came up with a detailed written confession of the satanic rituals he had purportedly conducted for years. He fired his lawyer and pleaded guilty on all charges. In the course of a number of additional sessions, the names of the other participants were brought to the fore. None of the other participants were prosecuted, as the evidence in their cases turned out to be totally unreliable. The claims of the daughters that they had had repeated abortions and that their bodies were covered with scars were refuted by a medical examination. No sign was found of the numerous bodies that, on their report, had been allegedly buried in their garden. Ingram was sent to jail solely on the basis of his signed confession. This was the first court case in which massive repression was alleged to have occurred not only in the victim, but also in the perpetrator. Richard Ofshe, a Pulitzer Prize winning writer,[1] who was brought in as an expert witness by the prosecution, received permission to interview Ingram (Ofshe, 1992). Impressed by the suggestive nature of the encounters between the pastor, the psychologist, and Ingram, Ofshe decided to conduct a clinical experiment. Before meeting with Ingram, he met with the daughters and asked them whether the sons had not also been involved in the rituals and whether on any occasion they had been made to perform brother–sister incest. The daughters denied this. Ofshe met with Ingram and told him that, as an investigator of charges involving satanic cults, he was reexamining the case, and wished to check if Ingram had not omitted some important material. He then asked Ingram whether his sons had ever been forced to commit incest with his daughters, to which Ingram replied in the negative. Ofshe then suggested that this might perhaps have occurred although neither Ingram nor his children remembered it. Like the psychologist and the pastor, Ofshe invited Ingram to meditate and pray for revelations on the issue of sister–brother incest. On the next day, Ingram came up with a detailed confession of occurrences of forced incest involving the sons and the daughters. Ofshe confronted him with his daughters' statements, but Ingram stood by his version. Ofshe's experiment, had shown that, with the "appropriate" process of inquiry, it was perfectly possible for Ingram to come to believe that he was guilty of acts he had not committed. After a few months, Ingram changed his mind and decided to recall his signed confession. It was too late. Ingram was in jail for 14 years until April 2003, when he received a pardon from the governor of the state ofWashington.[2]

7. Cure consists of the eradication of the hidden evil. In the religious demonic view, evil acts stem from evil roots, the ultimate source of which is the devil. The sinner can only be saved when the hidden roots are eliminated. In the psychological counterpart of this view, damaging symptoms and psychological complaints result from pathogens, whose source is almost invariably abuse and neglect. Again, a real cure is only possible if the pathogens is diagnosed and psychologically eliminated. This view has long overstepped the boundaries of professional psychology; many lay people have come to assume that all their problems have traumatic roots that they hope to uncover and eradicate.

There is a close link between this assumption and the "either–or" logic that is so typical of demonic thinking. If the ultimate source of all negative

---

[1]For publishing a disclosure of the criminal activities of Synanon, a group originally devoted to helping drug addicts kick the drug.

[2]A description of the proceedings together with the report of the medical examination of the daughters and some of the copious bibliography on the case can be found on the Internet site http://members.aol.com/ingramorg

acts is the devil, any partial solution or compromise would mean colluding with him. Partial improvements might then be actually worse than no solution at all, because the evil source within the soul would remain untouched and one would develop the dangerous illusion that things were better. The illusion of improvement would make one drop one's guard, thus allowing the devil to pursue his work undisturbed. For this reason, compromisers are often viewed by demonists as if they were in league with Satan. This process explains the tendency of witch hunts to spread exponentially; those that partake in "the conspiracy of silence" (the compromisers) are gradually viewed as no less guilty than the witches.

Similar processes may be observed in the psychological sphere. Attempts at mere amelioration or symptomatic relief are often viewed with suspicion, for the real problem is supposedly left untouched. Therapists who aim at such partial goals may be accused by other professionals of putting clients at risk by offering them merely symptomatic or cosmetic treatment. In the past, one of us, who offered hypnotic treatment for weight loss, was publicly charged with professional irresponsibility. This charge was made by a well-known therapist, who claimed that symptomatic treatment for weight problems might cause a schizophrenic outbreak. Fortunately, many professionals are now aware that "symptom substitution" is a myth (Bandura, 1969). Even so, "symptomatic treatment" is still usually frowned on as constituting an inferior kind of therapy. In addition, the pervasive influence of a putative conspiracy of silence has often been mentioned in psychological discourse. Professionals and lay persons alike have often been charged of abetting such a conspiracy in areas such as satanic cults and child abuse. Any skeptical stance, such as refusing to unconditionally accept as true the claims of adults that suddenly remembered they were sexually abused as children is often viewed as a repetition of the abuser's attempt to silence the victim.

An intriguing parallel can also be drawn between religious procedures of exorcism and psychological techniques for establishing contact with presumed multiple personalities in the individual ("alters" in the pop-psychological jargon), or for abreacting traumatic experiences. As in the religious procedures for contacting and expelling demons (e.g., Levack, 1992), psychological procedures for detecting traumatic experiences or contacting alters often begin with a ritualized inquiry. Hypnosis or *narcoanalysis* (i.e., the induction of a suggestive state by the use of a drug, such as sodium amytal or pentothal) have often been used to enable such procedures. Hypnotic techniques like *finger questioning* (in which the client is told that her fingers will move automatically signalizing "yes" and "no" in answer to the hypnotherapist's questions), *induced dreams* (in which the client is asked to let her mind wander and sink into a dreamlike state of experiencing), *age-regression* (in which the client is asked to experience time flowing backward until she is back at the age of supposed abuse), and *symptom-focusing* (in which the client is asked to focus on a particular symptom or body feeling and allow it to guide her back to the first time it appeared) are common tools for bringing the allegedly repressed memories back to consciousness. In conditions such as battle trauma, the induction of the traumatic experience can be abetted by the use of simulation methods that replicate the stimuli of combat, such as using a tape recorder with battle sounds. Sometimes the client reacts to these techniques by actually reliving the presumed or real traumatic experience or by impersonating one or more of her alters. At other times, the client reacts quietly, merely giving information by finger movements or verbal mutterings. The therapist usually encourages the client to vent emotions, as it is commonly believed that success stands in direct proportion to the intensity of emotional expression. When an alter is contacted, a dialogue with her often takes place and an attempt is made to have her agree to leave the host in peace in the future. Sometimes this is achieved through negotiation; the alter may then be thanked for services in allowing the client to survive the trauma and in calling attention to the hidden past. If, however, the alter is a representative of the abuser, the process is rather one of expulsion, resembling religious exorcism. Another similarity is the expectation that the repressed trauma or alter will tenaciously resist being exposed and expelled. This resistance is reflected in the person's acute suffering throughout the experience.

ONE VARIETY OF PSYCHODEMONIC NARRATIVE

In the religious demonic narrative, innocent people are possessed by demons and made into unwitting hosts who disseminate the rule of the forces of darkness. In order to escape detection and pursue their work undisturbed, the demons, who lodge within the individual, hide themselves as best they can (often even from the host). The disguise is helped out by a widespread cover-up, a conspiracy of silence, in which large sections of society participate, sometimes unwittingly. Many of these participants have been duped by satanic powers to disbelieve imputations of witchcraft and possession. Skepticism is thus one of Satan's mainstays. However, the demonic forces ultimately reveal themselves to the sharp and trained eyes of inquisitors, confessors, and exorcists. This discovery is then followed by the grim but holy work of examination, confession, exorcism, and purification, which necessarily involve pain. This pain is more than balanced by the hope of salvation, both of the infected individual and of the society of the faithful. Thus the fight against the forces of darkness and the hope of redemption go hand in hand. Actually, the intensity of this fight reflects the degree of apocalyptic tension; the more intense the fight, the greater the hope of imminent redemption. The missionary zeal of the antidemonic forces is thus not only corrective, but millenarian in scope (Cohn, 1975; Ginzburg, 1991).

In the presently most popular variety of psychodemonic narrative, the counterpart of the demonic host is the victimized carrier of psychodemonic implants, such as repressed traumatic experiences, the parents' negative internalized voices, or the perpetrators' programmed instructions. Their hidden wounds supposedly lead the one-time victims to subject others to a traumatization similar to the one they suffered. Psychological evil thus perpetuates itself very much like its demonic counterpart; yesterday's victim is tomorrow's perpetrator. Also similar to the traditional demonic narrative is the manner by which the psychodemonic implants hide themselves from view by numbing the person's mind, disguising themselves into their opposites, or dissociating themselves from consciousness. Only a highly trained eye can see through these disguises. Professional and social skepticism hinder this unmasking process, but the alert therapist may find an ally in the victim, who feels the need to break out from the imposed silence and speak out. Often, the truth-speaking voice within the client is actually the child within the adult who, as it were, comes back from banishment, and unmasks the culprits. In this narrative the therapist is often a one-time skeptic, whose disbelief is overturned by the revelations to which he or she is exposed. When this occurs, the therapist breaks out of the conspiracy of silence, which the therapist once unwittingly abetted, becoming instead the daring protector who provides the victim with the security needed to overcome inner repression and outer oppression. As in the traditional demonic story, the process of overcoming the trauma and getting rid of its implants is necessarily painful. The pain stems from the need to relive the original trauma, and from the horror experienced at the monstrous acts perpetrated by those closest to the victim. As the victim discovers all that was done to her and how she was forced to cooperate, the victim may sometimes go through a stage where she views herself as repulsive and contagious. The psychodemonic story thus includes a self-demonizing phase, which may be no less virulent than the demonization of the victim's significant others.

The common assumptions shared by the traditional and the psychological versions of the demonic narrative are so extensive that they may explain why the belief in satanic cults spread so quickly among therapists and the general public in the 1980s and 1990s; it is as if the psychodemonic interpretation had not satisfied the need for a totally evil source of suffering. There had to be a "real" satanic conspiracy behind it all! The satanic cult epidemic is a clear example of the aforementioned interaction between professional and popular psychology. In our view, the link between satanic abuse and multiple-personality-disorder was most likely forged in some rather peripheral professional circles. With the first books on the subject, however, it became clear that the story's popular appeal went beyond the authors' wildest expectations. The wide interest among the general public gradually fed back into professional circles. More and more therapists joined the dance; multiple-personality-disorder was increasingly diagnosed and accusations of satanic abuse mushroomed. The wave gradually subsided; therapists became less and less willing to openly declare their belief in satanic cults or to persuade their clients to sue their parents. The diagnosis of multiple-personality-disorder was replaced by that of the less colorful and risky dissociative disorder. The rage faded.

Before outlining the tragic assumptions, we want to stress that although the demonic view draws some of its inspiration from psychoanalysis, it is a far cry from the position of most psychoanalysts. Psychoanalysis certainly shares the assumption about the hidden roots of much of human suffering; however, it is the rare psychoanalyst who would endorse the belief that all suffering comes from evil, that there is a willful conspiracy of silence, or that a cure lies in an abreactive experience that frees the mind from its traumatic implants. Freud himself was philosophically and morally close to the tragic position, holding that suffering is an inevitable part of life and that the process of cure is one of recognizing and coming to terms with one's darker sides, rather than one of expelling them from the mind. Freud also rejected the assumption of basic innocence (Sulloway, 1979). Many theoreticians and therapists in the psychoanalytic tradition have, in addition, discarded the suspicious attitude toward the client that had characterized older generations of psychoanalysts. Kohut (1971, 1977) is probably the chief representative of a position that is very close to the tragic view, according to which even the most irrational-seeming aspects of the client's development actually represent significant achievements in her coping with a precarious life situation. In addition, influential figures like Spence (1982) and Schaffer (1983) contested the presumption of some analysts that they are possessed of an X-ray view of the client's unconscious that should prevail over the client's own experience and claims. These influential psychoanalysts have totally disconnected themselves from anything resembling a psychodemonic view.

THE TRAGIC VIEW

Tragic Assumptions

1. Suffering is an essential part of life. This seeming truism is the opposite of the basic demonic postulate (all suffering comes from evil). Viewing suffering as an essential part of life means that there is no party that can be held completely responsible for it. In addition, nothing can ever bring about the total elimination of suffering, which is simply the downside of human fallibility, vulnerability, and mortality. This view does not imply a passive position; improvements and self-protection are not only possible, but mandatory. The assumption that suffering is essential to life reflects an attitude that we would term *constructive fatalism.* Whereas the demonic view can be regarded as implying a millenarian attitude (extirpating evil will bring redemption), the position of constructive fatalism reflects a readiness to work for improvement while accepting the inherent limitations of the human condition.

In classical tragedy, suffering is depicted as the result of *fate.* This term denotes the confluence of factors by which circumstances and personality join hands to bring about the tragic outcome. Thus, in different circumstances, Macbeth's personality might have led to a better life. Likewise, a man with a constitution that differed from Macbeth's might, under the same circumstances, have remained untainted. Fate is not a personal force. It is neither good nor evil and has no intentions whatsoever. Fate is therefore as much the opposite of Satan as of God. We find that a concept like *fate,* or simply *bad luck* or *accident* could beneficially be used in psychotherapy as an antidote to the tendency to blame others or the self for the existence of suffering.

The understanding that in many situations, the end result lies not in one's hands can be both disheartening and liberating. In today's control-oriented culture, one tends to magnify the discouraging side; anything that implies lack of control is negatively connoted. We shall refer to the belief that control is always possible and desirable as *the illusion of control.* In contrast, we often find that people often react positively to the suggestion that their control is limited, sometimes expressing obvious relief at this possibility: "If it is not in my hands, why suffer?" This transition from the pain of control to the relief of acceptance is illustrated in a Biblical story about King David:

> The Lord struck the child that Uriah's wife bore to David, and it was very sick. David therefore begged God for the child; and David fasted, and went in, and lay all night on the earth. The elders of his house arose, and stood beside him, to raise him up from the earth; but he would not, neither did he eat bread with them. It happened on the seventh day, that the child died. The servants of David feared to tell him that the child was dead; for they said, Behold, while the child was yet alive, we spoke to him, and he didn't listen to our voice: how will he then vex himself, if we tell him that the child is dead! But when David saw that his servants were whispering together, David perceived that the child was dead; and David said to his servants, Is the child dead? They said, He is dead. Then David arose from the earth, and washed, and anointed

> himself, and changed his clothing; and he came into the house of the Lord, and worshiped; then he came to his own house; and when he required, they set bread before him, and he ate. Then said his servants to him, What thing is this that you have done? You did fast and weep for the child, while it was alive; but when the child was dead, you did rise and eat bread. He said, While the child was yet alive, I fasted and wept; for I said, Who knows whether the Lord will not be gracious to me that the child may live? But now he is dead, why should I fast? Can I bring him back again? I shall go to him, but he will not return to me. (*Samuel* II, 12)

The paradox inherent in the view that acceptance may be a positive force is one of the hallmarks of the tragic attitude. Interestingly, acceptance of fate does not preclude action. Thus people who are strict determinists in their outlook are not any less active and energetic than staunch believers in the freedom of the will. Schopenhauer and Spinoza are cases in point; if asked how they could be so active and resourceful, though they did not believe they could change the predetermined course of events, they might have replied: "Fate has made me so!"

Although modern psychology is usually identified with an optimistic ethos of change and control, this does not characterize the work of many influential psychologists. Freud, for instance, viewed suffering as inherent in the human condition and conflict as not only inescapable, but as basically unresolvable. To his mind, compromise solutions are all that can be ever had (Rieff, 1979; Sulloway, 1979). For many therapists, this fatalistic or pessimistic strain in Freud's worldview is a limitation to be overcome. Not so Mann (1973), a psychoanalyst who developed *time-limited-therapy.* For Mann, the ability to accept limitation and disappointment is the hallmark of the mature person. The hope that all problems can be solved and all goals achieved is what often puts people at loggerheads with existence. Time-limited-therapy is accordingly an intensive course in "constructive disappointment." The central theme of this kind of therapy is a formulation of the tragic conflict between the individual's dominant life wish and its inevitable frustration. Mann holds that any person's central wish is invariably frustrated because such wishes are basically insatiable. Thus, people who wish for personal security will find that they are never secure enough, those who strive for power will desire ever more power, and those who want romantic love will want love to be all the more romantic. Mann's time-limited-therapy lasts 12 sessions. This time limit involves a necessary disappointment, because the major conflict cannot be thoroughly discussed or analyzed (or, needless to say, solved) in such a short period of time. In addition, with only 12 sessions to go, separation is a therapeutic issue from the very start; no matter how comfortable the client may feel with her therapist, the shadow of the end is already present at the beginning. The bottom line of this "tragic therapy" is learning to accept the limitations of therapy and life. Mann was probably the first therapist who turned the tragic limitations of the human condition into a central therapeutic lever.

The value of acceptance as a therapeutic attitude has been highlighted by Stephen Hayes and his colleagues in their book, *Acceptance and Commitment Therapy* (Hayes, Strosahl, & Wilson, 1999). Contrary to the ruling ethos of control in Western culture, these authors have argued that accepting the far-reaching limitations of our hopes of control may well be the key to a better life. This acceptance leads to an attitude of "creative hopelessness," in which the individual becomes ready to strive for partial improvement without succumbing to the mirage of trying to control her own mental or physical state. The similarity between creative hopelessness and our own term, *constructive fatalism*, is obvious. The attitude of creative hopelessness is far from passive; Hayes and his colleagues stress that acceptance of the inevitable goes hand in hand with a clear commitment to ameliorative action. Like these authors, we put the dialectics of acceptance and action at the center of this book. We believe that tragic wisdom consists in achieving a synthesis between the two.

2. Bad acts often stem from positive qualities. This assumption specifically counters the demonic belief that links damaging acts to negative inner qualities. From a tragic perspective, even acts that carry the most negative consequences often stem from qualities that were or still are of positive value. These qualities, however, may have become rigidified or overextended, thus becoming disconnected from the changing circumstances. This assumption is illustrated by the concept of *hubris*, which plays a central role in classical tragedy; *hubris* refers to the ironic twist by which the very qualities that brought success may inspire the uncritical attitude that leads to disaster. It was Oedipus' kingly responsibility, his love of truth, and his certainty that he could solve any riddle (after all, he had defeated the Sphynx!) that brought him to attempt with all his might to find the secret that destroyed him. Hubris, though not necessarily under this name, is a well-known phenomenon; it is the refusal to accept one's limitations and the belief that one's positive qualities or "good star" are winning cards. It is when the individual forgets how limited is her power, how partial her knowledge, and how precarious her luck, that she is in the greatest danger. When the right way seems most clear and hesitations most petty, one may well be very close to the abyss. Viewing suffering as the result of hubris is thus the opposite of viewing it as the result of demonic forces.

The psychotherapeutic version of this assumption is the *principle of empathy*. Rigorously understood, this principle requires the therapist to assume that at the core of even the most irrational-seeming piece of behavior, there lies a humanly understandable adaptive striving. The secret of therapeutic empathy is precisely an unflinching attempt to find and express the positive human core behind all maladaptive behaviors. This attitude is a far cry from the mere passive echoing of the client's suffering. *Echo empathy* (e.g., "I understand how painful this is for you!" or "I see that you are really angry!"), with which therapeutic empathy is often equated, is a rather common and not necessarily psychotherapeutic experience. One can find it, for instance, at the barbershop, although the barber is no therapist. The therapeutic principle of empathy requires more than that. Thus, the therapist should focus on the human and adaptive side of the client's behavior, even when she or he behaves in a problematic or obstreperous manner (Kohut, 1977; Schaffer, 1983). This does not entail endorsing the client's acts wholesale, but viewing them as having an adaptive side, no less than a potentially harmful one. The negative side is actually the result of a rigidification or overextension of the positive side. Thus, instead of searching like the psychodemonic therapist for the negative essence behind even seemingly positive or neutral acts, the tragic-minded therapist looks for the positive human side behind the client's apparently negative manifestations.

3. The other is similar to us. Aristotle attributed the therapeutic and purifying (cathartic) value of tragedy to the fact that it arouses pity and fear; pity for the sufferings of the tragic figure and fear that a similar fate might be one's own. Tragic drama thus purifies through identification. To the extent that the tragic figure is viewed as a basically different person, the onlooker fails to understand, does not participate, and is not purified by the experience. The process of demonization works through disidentification—the other, who in our initial ignorance, seemed similar to us, is gradually seen as basically different. The catharsis of tragedy, in contrast, works through the transcendence of apparent otherness; we become Macbeth, Othello, Oedipus, or Medea.

To maintain the picture of the other as an hostile alien, one must assume that behind any seemingly positive or neutral acts, there lie negative intentions, motives, and feelings. The hidden is thus more real than the manifest. For the tragic mind, however, thoughts, feelings and acts are equally real. Reducing any of them to the status of an accident or an epiphenomenon, or turning any of the three into the handmaid of the other is a degradation of human fullness. Oedipus thinks, feels, and acts fully at every stage of his tragic career. To hold that the story "really" means that Oedipus was ruled by his unconscious and that his thoughts and acts were mere appendages to his repressed drives is, like all reductive thinking, a caricature.

The tragic attitude rejects the pervasive suspicion of the demonic outlook. In viewing the other as a human being, who is basically similar to us, and in attributing an equal reality status to her acts, thoughts, and feelings, we become free from the discounting stance that characterizes the demonizing interaction.

4. There is no outside privileged view into any person's experience. For the psychologically minded reader, this assumption can be very difficult to accept. Consider, however, that tragic identification becomes impossible if the outside viewer knows better than the tragic character what her "real" feelings are. Thus, if the outside viewer knew that Oedipus had really wished to marry his mother, or that Macbeth had really wanted to murder everybody, there would be no identification and no tragedy. The assumption of a privileged view into the other's experience is thus fatal to tragedy and to any form of empathic identification. In contrast, this assumption is essential to the demonic view; without demon doctors, or experts, who are possessed of an X-ray view of the other's soul, the whole demonic or psychodemonic enterprise would collapse.

To identify with the other, it is necessary to follow him step by step. One meets the witches along with Macbeth, listens to their alluring prophecies, fears for their horrid consequences, hesitates before the deed, gets drawn in the whirlpool of bloody acts, and, gradually, evolves feelings of horror, disgust, and despair. Of course the viewer knows the story beforehand, but she never knows better than Macbeth what Macbeth's moment-to-moment thoughts, wishes, and feelings are. Even Tiresias, the blind prophet, knows what is to come, but knows no better than Oedipus what Oedipus is experiencing. If one knew better, identification would break down. This is true for psychotherapists as well as for husbands, wives, parents, and children; it is impossible to identify, if one believes to be in possession of a privileged look into the hidden recesses of the other's mind. Empathy that is predicated on the belief, "I know better than you what you really feel!" is, in this view, only a presumptive empathy.

An external observer may of course have a broader context in mind, more experience of life's circumstances, or better hunches about the future: however, the assumption that one knows the other's inner experience better than her may lead to the perversion of all dialogue. What is, for instance, the meaning of the following statement that is often made to male clients: "You are unconsciously attracted to men." Even if the recipient of this message eventually became an homosexual, he could legitimately contest the presence of feelings of attraction in the present. From a tragic perspective, feelings are felt, thoughts are thought, and motives incline. One is thus never entitled to say, "This is what you *really* feel!" Therapists can, of course, offer new formulations, draw attention to new facts, or put events in a new context. However, they cannot claim to have an X-ray view of the other's feelings or memories. This understanding is slowly gaining ground among psychotherapists. Thus, forms of therapy that expressly discard all pretension to a privileged look into the client's inner experience have gained considerable ground in recent years (e.g., Hoffman, 1993; White & Epston, 1990).

The pervasiveness of the belief that one can know better than the other what she "really" feels testifies to the immense impact of some forms of psychological thinking on modern culture. It takes considerable effort to understand that an assumption is at all at work on this issue. And yet, the belief about a privileged view may be no more than a well-rooted habit of mind; one believes strongly to be able to read into the other's mind, but she believes otherwise. The indignation she voices at one's presumptive knowledge, far from justifying one's claims to that knowledge, may attest only to their offensive nature. The anger is, to our mind, justified; any claim to a privileged view entails a lack of respect to the individual's inner experience. We would venture that much of the hard feelings that accompany what is termed *resistance* in psychotherapy has to do with this justified indignation at the therapist's presumptive privileged view. This is also true for the anger experienced by many a spouse or an adolescent at the assertions of spouse or parent concerning their "real" feelings. True, spouses and adolescents may also behave indignantly when they are caught in a lie. And yet, the interaction is a different one; the indignation here is usually a conscious effort to maintain the lie or to stop the other's attempts to force a confession. Not so the indignation against the mind reader; this is a defense of one's right to possess one's feelings.

In therapy, taking this assumption seriously means that the therapist will guard herself against a tendency to let her own view of the client's experience prevail on the client's. The therapist may give words to what she or he thinks the client is feeling. The therapist may also be able to achieve good formulations, perhaps even better than those of the client (after all, poets have done this throughout the ages; formulated the reader's feelings better than the reader). Yet, the validity of the therapist's attempts is conditioned by the client's inner assent. This rule is not easy to follow, particularly given the ingrained professional habits to the contrary. The potential gain, however, is significant; therapists can reduce their psychodemonic slips and mind-invasive practices. We believe that the therapeutic dialogue (and any other dialogue), far from being impoverished, would be thereby enriched.

5. Radical solutions often increase suffering. The greatest tragedies often come from the greatest dreams. Attempts to eradicate evil are often accompanied by the feeling that redemption is at hand. Paradoxically, the very attempt to end suffering by cutting off its putative source may prove devastating. Tragedy as an artistic form gives expression to this fateful irony;

it describes the protagonist's decisive venture that, instead of redeeming, destroys. A similar irony may also characterize many real-life tragedies, in which the split of good and evil and the suspicion of concealment engender a crusading zeal. The resulting militant attitude more often than not badly worsens the situation. In effect, the demonic view in personal relations amounts to a conspiracy theory at the individual level. People are not very often killed by it, but the suffering it causes suffices to shatter innumerable individuals and families.

The principled preference of root treatments to treatments that are disparagingly termed *cosmetic* can be highly problematic. In one of our cases, a young woman pressed her parents for a radical treatment for acne by a very extensive plastic surgery. With the help of the family physician and a talented cosmetician, the parents and the therapist succeeded in making her accept a program of symptomatic and cosmetic improvement instead. We regard this case as a therapeutic success. Along these lines, we try in the next chapter to bring the discipline of *therapeutic cosmetics* to a honorable standing. Actually, our work in this direction is far from original. In the history of psychotherapy, the exclusiveness of cure as the therapeutic goal par excellence has gradually given way to the more modest goals of reducing subjective discomfort, achieving symptomatic and functional improvement, and learning to live with one's limitations (goals that were caricaturized in the phrase, "I still wet my bed, but now I am proud of it!"). The pioneers in this trend were probably the behavior therapists who criticized the pejorative connotation of the term, *symptomatic treatment* by showing, for instance, that behavioral treatment of symptoms, far from causing "symptom substitution," often leads to a *ripple effect*, in which improvements in untreated areas usually result from a localized symptomatic improvement (Bandura, 1969). Also within the psychoanalytic field, a change in this direction can be felt. As mentioned, the evolution of time-limited-therapy legitimized a mix of partial improvement and acceptance of limitations as an appropriate goal for psychotherapy (Mann, 1973). Perhaps no one went further in this direction then the followers of the *solution oriented* approach. De Shazer (1985), for instance, proposed that the goal of psychotherapy should be the minimum improvement that the client would regard as significant. The rhetorics of "real-cure" are, however, very much alive in therapeutic discourse, particularly in its pop-psychological manifestations. We would venture that these rhetorics become manifest especially where psychodemonic assumptions are at their most active.

6. The ubiquity of suffering requires acceptance, compassion and consolation. In Western culture, with its ruling ethos of control, the virtues of acceptance, compassion, and consolation are often viewed as reflecting an attitude of passivity and resignation. In addition, compassion is viewed as condescending[4], and consolation as involving a sham substitute for real solutions. In modern eyes, cultural forms that abet the tragic triad of acceptance, compassion, and consolation are usually viewed as inferior. The very need for these virtues reflects the inability to achieve the level of technical progress or the depth of cure that would render them unnecessary. In the traditional demonic outlook, acceptance, compassion and consolation are viewed as especially misplaced when directed at the objects of suspicion. These attitudes are then interpreted as resulting from satanic deception, whose only goal is to diminish the believers' zeal. Thus, in the treatise on witches, *Malleus Maleficarum*, which became the handbook of the inquisition, the faithful were warned against any misplaced compassionate stance toward witches; such a stance could only be inspired by the devil and would amount to the worst possible sin short of witchery proper (Nesner, 1999).

Acceptance, compassion, and consolation are crucial stages in the emotional pilgrimage of the tragic figure. Some of the highest points in tragic drama are the mellow moments when the protagonists' acceptance transforms the experience of fate from that of an antagonizing to that of an embracing power. Thus Lear to Cordelia in their way to prison:

> Come, let's away to prison:
>
> We two alone will sing like birds i' th' cage:
>
> When thou dost ask me blessing, I'll kneel down
>
> And ask of thee forgiveness: so we'll live,
>
> And pray, and sing, and tell old tales, and laugh
>
> At gilded butterflies, and hear poor rogues
>
> Talk of court news; and we'll talk with them too,
>
> Who loses and who wins, who's in, who's out,

[4]Some distinguish "compassion" from "pity," viewing only "pity" as condescending. In the past, however, such a distinction was not usually made. Thus, Othello, explaining how Desdemona came to love him, "She loved me for the dangers I had passed/ And I loved her that she did pity them" (Othello, I, iii).

As if we were God's spies: and we'll wear out

In a walled prison, pacts and sects of great ones

That ebb and flow by th' moon. (*King Lear*, V, iii)

Such a concentrate of acceptance and consolation deserves the most in compassionate participation by the audience. This triad of attitudes has been deemed of yore to be most helpful to helpers and sufferers alike. It is therefore surprising how little attention it has received in the psychotherapeutic literature[5]. The lack, however, is beginning to be remedied. An important step in this direction was the publication of Hayes et al.'s (1999) aforementioned *Acceptance and Commitment Therapy*. The authors likened people's attempts to eradicate their own negative mental states to the efforts of someone trapped in a hole trying to get out by digging. Suppression attempts, however, will stay on, so long as the negative states of mind are viewed by the individual as totally unacceptable. Attempts to control these states of mind may then end by taking up all the person's energies, becoming solidified into concrete negative entities. However, once the individual understands that no absolute solution is available, a readiness to endure may begin to evolve that often affects the negative emotions in a positive way. Of course, the negative experiences do not simply go away as one stops the attempts to suppress them. However, they becomes more fluid, they ebb and they flow, and the person suffers less. The book is a treasure trove of metaphors, exercises, and simulations that help evolve a flexible attitude of acceptance and a readiness to endure. And yet, far from furthering passive resignation, the authors are staunch ameliorators. Their ameliorative stance is expressed, for instance, in their attempt to foster in the client an attitude of commitment to goals. The proper kind of commitment, however, has a tragic tone, for it involves acceptance of one's limitations. Actually, the authors say, one cannot commit oneself to success, but only to go on trying. This book is probably the most detailed example to date of an ameliorative tragic stance in psychotherapy. In a later chapter, we try to add our own contribution to the triad of tragic attitudes by presenting some ideas on the neglected virtue of consolation.

[5]"Acceptance" has been often discussed as the appropriate therapeutic attitude toward the client. However, acceptance of own's own limitations and acceptance of the limits of improvement have received far less attention.

CASE 4[6]

After having concluded his second year in computer sciences with high marks, Ralph felt he had no energy or desire to continue studying. In the two courses of therapy he had been through, Ralph had felt accepted and understood, but did not think he had been helped. After telling his disappointed mother that he would not go back to the university, he asked her for money to continue therapy. She agreed.

Ralph made no eye contact and his voice and posture gave the impression of someone who was talking to himself. He felt he was a talentless fake. He said he had an enormous need for approval, but at the same time he dismissed every encouragement as worthless. His teachers and classmates thought he was smart but they had no idea of the trouble he had even with the easiest assignment. All the talents in the family had fallen to his older sister; she was the brilliant academic his mother had always wished him to be. She was also pretty, sociable and happily married.

Ralph's mother was an art teacher. She and his father had divorced when Ralph was 13 years old and the father had immediately remarried. Ralph described his mother as a controlling and critical person; his father was generous and easygoing, although the relationship with his new wife kept these qualities at bay. The mother had tried to warn Ralph that his continuing attachment to his father was a mistake. Ralph would eventually discover that the father had never cared for him. The mother was sure that the father would not leave Ralph one cent after his death. Ralph felt that her hatred for his father blinded her and distorted also her relationship to himself. Ralph believed he was depressed and had no self-esteem because his mother had never loved or appreciated him. She had only wanted him to fulfill her dreams or to be a replicate of his sister. His earliest memories were of mother's coldness when he disappointed her. As he grew, her demands became more and more aggressive. She never encouraged him when he was in pain; on the contrary, she would then become most caustic. To top it all, the mother denied her negative feelings even to herself. However, in the very tone of her denial, he detected her revulsion. Being rejected and having the rejector deny her rejection were the source of all his troubles.

> *Both Ralph and his mother blamed another person for their sufferings: Ralph blamed his mother and the mother blamed Ralph's father. Ralph felt that his suffering was fully accounted for by his mother's rejection; she had been as rejecting as he was miserable. The demonic tone of this attri-*

[6]The case is in normal print and our comments in italics.

bution was enhanced by Ralph's contention the mother was in denial concerning her feelings toward him. The accusations of Ralph and his mother led to mutual escalation; each side attempted to convince the other of his or her view, and when the other remained unconvinced, each side doubled their efforts. This escalatory spiral is typical of interactions ruled by a demonic view.

Ralph said that the mother's behavior exposed the lies in her declarations. She said she had no expectations from him, but went on expecting the utmost. Because of his threats that he would stop studying, she had learned to react as if a mark of "B" was an achievement. But he knew she did not really think so. Neither did he. Furthermore, he did not feel he deserved even the Bs he was getting.

In the psychodemonic world, nothing is what it seems. Declared acceptance is no acceptance, satisfaction with "B" is no satisfaction, and even the "B" marks are not what they seem. The hypothesized negative underlying reality invalidates all positive events.

Ralph lived by himself but came to his mother's house every Friday. These weekly meetings were punctuated by bouts of mutual blaming. Ralph would blame her for her lack of love and she would blame him for picking on her to take revenge for imaginary ills. Recently, Ralph had told her that he would not come to the Passover meal. He said it was pointless for him to come because his sister would get all the love, he would get depressed, and destroy the festiveness of the occasion anyway. In the end, after the mother asked him repeatedly, he agreed to come. He arrived in a dark mood and, noticing the mother's displeasure, asked her whether she would not have liked it better it if he had not come. She said, "Yes!" This hurt him even more; she was owning up to her hatred for him! If she could have had it her way, she would have preferred to keep him out! Now he would get her to confess her real feelings! He started arguing with her, and found that the way she argued with him was the concrete proof of all his contentions.

The mother was put in a "damned if you do, damned if you don't" paradox; whether she said "yes" or "no" to Ralph's baiting question, she would be found guilty. We call this the witch's paradox; *the choice is given the "witch" to prove her innocence by the ordeal of water (being held underwater for a few minutes); if she comes out alive, her guilt is established and she is burnt at the stake; if she drowns, she shows her innocence, but is dead anyway.*

Only in his therapies had Ralph received confirmation of how deeply he had been rejected. The last therapist had been so cogent in this view that Ralph had found himself arguing that the mother had not been that bad after all!

The therapist inquired about the mother's occasional positive reactions and about the circumstances in which they occurred. Ralph said she would behave sufferably toward him when he felt well, but she became extremely rejecting when he became depressed. He added disparagingly that the mother claimed she was only trying to shake him out of his depression. The therapist said the mother seemed very threatened by his depression; she was reacting as if in a panic.

> *The demonic view is essentialist and black and white; the mother's inner attitude can be either loving or rejecting—there is no middle ground. The tragic way of thinking is contextual, shaded, and many-sided; the mother could, depending on circumstance, be more accepting or more rejecting. Moreover, what looked like rejection might be a panic reaction to Ralph's depression. The therapist attempted to enable a shift from a demonic to a tragic description; the mother's reactions, although painful to Ralph, might be understandable when taken in context.*

Gradually a change occurred in Ralph's focus of attention during the sessions, and he started talking about his mother's life. Her younger brother had dropped out of school and, later on, left work. The parents had always thought him delicate and sensitive, so they let him stay at home, hoping he would pull himself together. Instead, his depression deepened. He worked only occasionally, became withdrawn, and lived with his mother until the present day. He was not the only depressed person in the family. The mother's father had gone through a number of depressive episodes and had been medicated for years. The therapist wondered whether Ralph had not also been touched by this depressive family strain. Ralph agreed; he had always been sad and had repeatedly contemplated suicide. The therapist asked whether this depressive tendency might not have sharpened the mother's reactions; faced with a child who reminded her of her own brother and father, she might have felt an acute need to prevent the dreaded outcome. The mother's pushiness might thus be understandable in its context. Although intrigued by this possibility, Ralph was not ready to accept it; a tragic redescription of the mother would have to await more favorable circumstances.

Although Ralph at this time refused to have a joint session with the mother (in his previous therapies, such sessions had proved disastrous), he agreed that the therapist could meet with her alone. The following dialogue repeated itself in various forms in the three sessions the therapist had with her:

Mother: He wants attention and he wants revenge. He takes the martyr's position to punish me for all the ills I supposedly caused him. He sees only the negative side of things. That justifies him in blaming and in giving up. Whenever something good happens, he focuses so much on the negative, that in the end he must give up. His pessimism is just an excuse to shake off responsibility. He will destroy any positive chances, only to go on blaming, complaining, and then giving up. The moment he enters the house, looking like someone who has just come from his own funeral, I know what is in store for me. I am always the guilty one: I never loved him, I never accepted him, I have always preferred his sister.

Therapist: How do you react to his accusations?

Mother: I try to show him that it is not so. That I love him just as much as I love her. But he won't accept that!

Therapist: I believe he is wrong in his conclusion, but maybe he discerns something that is there, in the way you have been expressing your care for him. I can imagine that the interaction that developed between you two, given his constant sadness and your fears, should have been quite different from the one between you and your daughter. Maybe Ralph interpreted this as lack of love.

The therapist proposed an alternative to the mother's right/wrong dichotomy concerning Ralph's opinion of her: his conclusion might be wrong, but the inner experience understandable. This antidemonic tactic will be considered in detail in chapter 3.

Mother: What do you mean?

Therapist: I guess you had it easier with your daughter. He was a difficult child, often miserable, angry, and irritable. You could not but react differently to him.

Mother: But he thinks I *caused* his depression!

Therapist: Yes, he thinks so, and may also think so in the future. However, we know that depression has many causes; his early experiences might be one of them, but probably not the most important. Was he very different as a child than he is now?

Mother: No, he was always sad and angry. And always very sensitive to rejection from other kids, from the kindergarten teacher, from everyone. He was always unsure, even when he got high marks.

Therapist: So he was like that from a very early age. He was frequently in pain and you felt understandably helpless and frustrated. I guess that with your family history, you were bound to be badly shaken by Ralph's depressive tendency. Worry, frustration, and even anger were bound to arise. And how would Ralph react? With frustration and anger! This cycle was probably very hard both for you and for him.

Mother: Does he understand this?

Therapist: No, and I am afraid he won't, at least for quite a while. The depressed person is incapable of seeing more than the pain. When a dentist drills your tooth you cannot think very much about others; only the pain matters. So, there is little chance of Ralph's viewing things differently now.

Mother: What can be done?

Therapist: I am not sure. The fact is that your attempts to convince him that you love him the same as his sister never help. Maybe you could say to him that you actually were tenser with him, which of course is true. Saying that he is right in his perception doesn't mean that you are to blame.

Mother: I am afraid of his reaction. He might rave if I accepted that I was always tense with him.

Therapist: Maybe Ralph will find it hard to hear this, but at least he will get confirmation from you that his feelings were not totally baseless.

The mother felt that she needed the therapist's presence to be able to say that. Ralph, however, still refused to a joint session. Even so, the tension in her relationship with Ralph began to subside.

Ralph found a job in a supermarket. Initially the mother was angry that instead of going back to the university Ralph was again following his "self-destructive" bent *(The belief in a "self-destructive" drive that acts in opposition to the host's better knowledge is a typical demonic construct).* The therapist said that Ralph's decision might be a reasonable one. His chief problem now was not studying, but his tendency to give up in conflict situations. The new job might give Ralph a chance to experiment with better alternatives. The therapist pledged himself before the mother to help Ralph use the new situation as a means to this end. The mother stopped nudging Ralph about his decision. This led to a further drop in the tension between the two. By and by, Ralph agreed to a joint session.

At the beginning of the session, Ralph sat gloomy and silent. Gradually, the mother opened up. She said she felt that she was a total failure as a mother. All her hopes that she would be able to help Ralph out of his troubles caused only more pain. Nothing she ever did seemed to help. For years, Ralph had said that her relation to her daughter had been a different one. She had always denied this. The mother had thought it over, however, and thought that, in a sense, he had been right. It was not that she loved him less. But she was afraid of him. She did not mean this as an accusation, but as an acknowledgment. She cared for him as much as for his sister, but the relationship was different. It was harder, tenser, less pleasant. It was true that she was angry. The anger came out of her sense of failure and frustration. It was true that she had always had high expectations from him. She could not avoid to have expectations, even though she knew it did not help. She would then grow tense and her tenseness would betray itself to Ralph. So she always felt she was under a looking glass, and even worse, under a microscope. After a short silence, Ralph said, very quietly, that he really looked at her under a microscope. Surprisingly, both laughed. The mother then said that she also looked at him under a microscope.

> *The mother's report reflects an evolving tragic perspective; neither had negative motives, instead, the trouble between them seemed to grow tragically out of good intentions. It thus became possible for the mother to speak of her damaging reactions without giving or taking blame.*

Ralph's relationship with his mother continued slowly improving. But then, a sad event occurred that put the relationship under bad strain—Ralph's father died. Ralph decided he would sit *Shivah*[7] for his father in his apartment. At the end of the *Shivah*, Ralph seemed to be sinking into a depression. He did not go back to work, refused to leave the house, and obsessed about the past, the divorce, and the irreparable damage the mother had done to him. The mother, who had brought him food everyday during the *Shivah*, started to pressure him to pull himself together. She then mentioned, once again, the taboo subject of the father's will; Ralph would soon find out what the father had left him! She tried to shake Ralph out of his depression and said she would not condone him in his self-pity. Ralph accused her of being insensitive and rejecting. He tried to stop her physically from leaving and demanded that she say openly she had never cared for him. She slapped him and left. He sank further and further in resentment. The demonic cycle seemed to have reasserted itself.

A week after the clash with his mother, Ralph found out that she had been right; the father had left him nothing! At first Ralph could not believe it. Little by little, however, he found a way to hold on to the view that the father had loved him, by coming to think of him as a weak man who had been unable to hold his own against the two strong women in his life. In the therapy, the mother's ill-timed mention of the father's will and her loss of control were discussed and reframed in a tragic direction; the mother had first tried to prepare Ralph for the bitter truth and then got into a panic when she saw him sinking into a depression. At this time, Ralph said to the therapist his refusal to participate in the routine psychological lynching of his mother had always intrigued him in a positive way. He added: "After all, who wants to have a monster for a mother?"

[7]Shivah is the traditional Jewish week of mourning.

Ralph's stance toward his mother and particularly the mother's stance toward him softened up. Occasionally, he would still grow apathetic and the mother would rave. But the cutting edge was no longer there. The mother even succeeded by her occasional ravings to achieve some positive outcomes; she convinced Ralph to take antidepressant medication (the therapist had failed to do so), and to buy himself an apartment. Even Ralph admitted, in the therapy, that his mother's "tantrums" had had a positive effect in these cases. After 2 years, Ralph went back to the university and finished his studies.

Chapter 3

The Antidemonic Dialogue in Therapy

Let us make it clear that we are not offering a new "tragic therapy" to join the hundreds of methods with which the field is already flooded. Nor are we presenting a gloomy and pessimistic outlook, as might be implied by the term *tragic*. We rather try to systematize the facets of a dialogue that may appear in any therapy, whenever the therapist tries to mitigate the demonic attitudes that are reflected in the client's words. The client, of course, does not speak in explicit demonic terms. However, the outlines of what we term *the demonic view* may gradually become manifest, as the client describes the problem, herself or himself, intimate others, and the solutions hoped for. The picture that emerges is then black and white, the tone suspicious and hostile, the attitude militant and radical, and the goals totalist and redemptive.

Our aim is not the ambitious one of replacing, in the client's mind, the demonic with the tragic view; uprooting beliefs is a demonic and not a tragic goal. We are satisfied with the more modest goal of inserting a wedge in the perfect closure of the demonic outlook. If the client becomes able to develop a more shaded picture, if the search for radical solutions is tempered, if room is given to inner voices that were previously suppressed, if suspicion lessens, and signs of compassion appear—then the client will be moving away from a demonic attitude and closer to a tragic one. In all this we try to help the client refocus his attention from the problem's assumed negative core ("the enemy within") to circumstantial aspects, which may be more amenable to small, but cumulative modifications. The antidemonic dialogue is thus invariably a partial one. The therapist tries to modify some of the demonic aspects in the client's attitude, without grappling with the demonic view head-on.

The term, tragic, in this book has not the usual connotation of "tragedy" in the sense of "disaster" or "cruel fate" (such as in the newspaper headline, "Tragedy in the Village: Man Murders Parents and Commits Suicide"). Therefore the emotional tone of the therapeutic dialogue we are proposing is not at all gloomy and pessimistic. Our use of tragedy refers to the artistic and philosophical meaning of the term. In this sense the tragic and the comic come into the world bound together. The ancient mask that represents theater shows a tragic profile on one side and a comic one on the other. In the theatrical events in classic Greece, a trilogy of tragedies was always concluded by a comedy. In Shakespeare, the tragic and the comic are inseparably intertwined. Similarly, the tragic view in therapy often has a comic dimension. In a conversation with a dying client, one of us was surprised that he and the client were laughing aloud, although they were talking about the impending end. The therapist then remarked, "The fact that we are laughing does not mean that the situation is funny!" And again the two burst out laughing.

The demonic outlook comes to view in various facets: in the description of the problem ("there is something inside me that destroys me"), in the description of self and other ("he is a sadist, and I am a masochist"), in the interpretation of actions ("she does it in order to humiliate me"), in the definition of goals ("we want a root treatment, once and for all"), and in the evaluation of progress ("this was merely a cosmetic improvement"). Before dealing with these different facets, we want to highlight three tools of any therapeutic dialogue and of the antidemonic dialogue in particular: reframing, questions, and metaphors.

REFRAMING

Reframing in the psychotherapeutic literature refers to any therapeutic activity that changes the relationship between the client's mental map and the events in his life circumstances. For instance, a phenomenon that was viewed as purely negative may be reframed as having also a positive side. The specific acts that can lead to reframing are many: (a) a broadening or narrowing of the problem's definition, (b) a change in the dividing lines of the client's conceptual map, (c) a change in the salience of different life areas, (d) a refocusing of attention from failures to achievements, and so forth. These changes lead to new feelings, goals, and actions, hopefully in a positive direction. In this section, we focus on one specific means of reframing that can have a high impact either in a demonic or an antidemonic direction: the assembling and dismantling of conceptual units[1].

---

[1]Our discussion of this subject was much influenced by the work of the Belgian philosopher and jurist, Chaim Perelman (1982.). In psychology, Kelly (1955) evolved a comprehensive theory, assessment procedure, and therapeutic dialogue, focusing on the assembling and dismantling of concepts.

These rather cumbersome terms refer to something quite familiar. The dismantling of a concept is exemplified in the phrase, "Your love is only words but no feeling" (the concept, *love*, is dismantled into the contrasting pair: "love as words" versus "love as feeling"). The assembling of a conceptual unit is exemplified in the phrase: "For me, your looking at other women like that is the same as inviting them to go to bed with you" (the distinct concepts, "looking at women like that" and "inviting them to go to bed " are assembled in the implied concept of *marital infidelity*).

The demonic view makes use of conceptual dismantling in order to split the world into good and evil, us and them, friend and enemy. There is of course nothing wrong with the use of such polarized concepts per se. We would perish if we could not distinguish friend from foe, or food from poison. Demonic polarization, however, involves a rigid, suspicious, and hostile frame of mind. Consider the following contrasting statements: (a) "The overcontrolling mother is particularly elusive, because her control comes disguised as love," and (b) "Even the greatest villain has a grain of good inside him." Both quotes are similarly constructed. In both the central concept (respectively, the overcontrolling mother and the villain) is dismantled into two contrasting aspects: overt and covert, and positive and negative. However, the attitude of the first quote is demonic, that of the second, antidemonic.

In dismantling a concept, two different aspects are highlighted so as to create a contrasting pair. Psychology is rife with such polarities: subjective/objective, process/content, conscious/unconscious, body/mind, cognitive/emotional, nature/nurture, and so on. This dismantling activity is usually so automatic that is hardly noticed, so much so that the dualities are assumed to be really present in the world. By ignoring that the dismantling is the work of one's mind and assuming instead that it is a faithful reflection of reality, one tends to view any different conceptual map as an erroneous or even perverse distortion.

Dismantling is an important tool for settling contradictions. For instance, the quote about the overcontrolling mother deals with two apparently contradictory motives—caring versus control. The conflict raises the question, "Which of the two is the real motive?" The dismantling of the concept into "seemingly caring" versus "actually controlling" resolves the paradox by defining the control as "deeper" and therefore more real. There is an obvious link between this particular dismantling and the demonic assumption that the hidden is more real than the manifest. In contrast, the second quote is rather antidemonic: the grain of good is seen as no less real than the wickedness. The dismantling in this quote is not of the sort "*either* good *or* evil" but "*both* good *and* evil." Usually, the tragic view tends to dismantlings of a "both–and" kind, whereas the demonic view tends to dismantlings of an "either–or" kind. Additional examples of "either–or" demonic dismantlings are, "You are either with me or against me!" "This is a life-and-death battle!" "Make it or break it!" "Now I will know whether she loves me or not!" In psychotherapeutic parlance, this tendency to extreme either-or formulations has also been termed *splitting.*

In the antidemonic dialogue, the therapist may propose reframes that mitigate the client's demonic dismantlings, by changing them from "either–or" to "both–and" formulations. For instance, a father criticizes his adolescent son who refuses to take a stand in his favor in his divorce struggle: "He has to decide! He is either with me or against me! If he is against me—I don't want to see him again!" The therapist might offer a more positive dismantling by saying, "Maybe he is against you in his thoughts, but with you in his feelings," or "Maybe he is torn between you two and therefore he is both with you and against you."

The phrase, "Even the worst villain has a grain of good inside him", suggests an additional therapeutic advantage of antidemonic dismantlings of the "both–and" kind. It is common knowledge that a person can best profit from criticism if he feels it is voiced out of respect and appreciation. A mother complained that her children showed her no respect, though she always gave them unconditional love and fulfilled their every wish. One of us told the mother,

> I am sure your children get much emotional nourishment out of this. However, you may be depriving them of a vital experience; children need to feel they lack something in order to learn how to cope with frustration. Maybe by giving so fully, you cause them "a lack in lacking." This lacking may be missing in their lives.

In this reframe, the mother's giving is dismantled into a positive component (emotional nourishment) and a negative one (depriving them of the necessary experience of lacking). The mother's behavior is *both* emotionally nourishing *and* depriving. The negative component is easier to accept, because it is joined to the positive one.[2]

If the dismantling of conceptual units helps one to see different sides in something that previously looked unitary, the assembling of conceptual units may help to view something that previously looked independent as part of a larger whole. The angry father in the divorce example said of his son, "The fact that he is not willing to say I am right shows that he has no respect for me!" The father is mapping the son's specific act ("not willing to

[2] We discussed this kind of dismantling in our book, *Constructing Therapeutic Narratives* (Omer & Alon, 1997).

say I am right") into a larger negative whole, namely, his lack of respect. This mapping amplifies the negative significance of the son's behavior. The therapist can propose an alternative conceptual unit: "The fact that he stands up for himself probably shows his basic trust in your relationship." This anti-demonic rejoinder reframes the son's assertiveness as part of a larger positive whole—his trust in the relationship.

CASE 5

Rachel and Gordon, who met each other in their forties, sought therapy at Gordon's initiative because of a "sexual problem": They both thought Rachel's level of desire for him was low. Rachel, however, was happy with the love between them and minimized the importance of sexuality in the relationship. She felt her love for Gordon, in spite of the low sexuality, was far better than the loveless sexuality she had experienced with others. Gordon, however, feared that Rachel's lack of passion reflected repressed feelings of hostility toward men and rejection of him as a man. He made Rachel's lack of desire into a part of the larger whole (rejection of him as a man). The equation "lack of desire equals rejection" led him to make an either–or demand from Rachel and from the therapy: "If we can solve the sex problem—good! If not—we must separate." The lack of sexuality thus received a psychodemonic significance, representing all the hidden negative facets in the relationship. Gordon's ultimatum, sex or separation, also reflects a typical demonizing attitude: Only by getting rid of the demon (Rachel's putative rejection and her hostility toward men) could their relationship survive.

The therapist talked to the couple at length about their life together and learned they both enjoyed physical contact, did a lot of hugging and kissing, and enjoyed eating, drinking, and traveling together. They also had a joint pleasure in the visual arts, to which they devoted a large part of their free time. They both agreed this was the best relationship either of them had ever had. The therapist summarized his assessment as follows:

> I am impressed there is a lot of love between you. I see too that your sexuality is very important to you. True, it is far from perfect, but on the other hand you have a great deal of something that other people would envy you for—sensuality. Each of you separately and the two of you together are very sensual people. This is something far broader than sexuality. It refers to the pleasurable meeting of the body and the senses with the world. Sensuality can flourish even without explicit sexuality, while plain and mechanical sexuality can be totally devoid of sensuality. I suggest that for the moment, we put aside all direct attempts to influence your sexuality; just as you can't force yourself to fall asleep you

> can't force yourself to have sexual desire. Let's try instead to enrich the broader area where you have such an advantage—the area of sensuality, which to my mind is the more meaningful of the two. Let us hope that as this deepens, your sexual life may eventually gain, but even if it does not, your life will be richer.

This dismantling of sexuality into sexuality and sensuality was an antidemonic formulation, for instead of focusing exclusively on the deep negative significance of low sexuality, it highlighted the couple's positive sensuality. As usual in sex therapy, the couple was asked to avoid direct sexual contact and focus on actions such as mutual massage, sauna, bathing together, and so on. In the sessions, the therapist tried again and again to dismantle the equation, lack of sexuality equals rejection, and brought numerous counterexamples of *both* love *and* absence of sex, such as Plato's *Symposium*, *Dante and Beatrice*, and *Heloise and Abelard*. For this cultivated and art-loving couple, these examples were helpful in making them appreciate what was special about their relationship.

In individual meetings with Rachel, the therapist learned that in the past she had had relationships that were mostly sexual and in which she had felt a lot of desire. She viewed those relationships as "sluttish," but saw her relationship with Gordon as "pure." She described herself as suffering from "the complex of the Madonna and the whore." For her, the situation was strictly either–or: She was either sluttish or pure. The therapist suggested that in a state of relaxation, she bring to memory stimulating sexual events from the past. She did that and found that her sluttish memories were arousing, although she felt no personal longing for her one-time partners. The therapist suggested she use those memories when she was with Gordon in order to arouse herself. She objected: "I don't want to contaminate our relationship. It is almost like bringing another man into our bed. It is an act of exploitation and a betrayal." The therapist answered, "If the idea does not suit you we will throw it away. But if you can use your sluttish memories to warm up your present love, and thereby enrich it—then that might be a positive exploitation and a good betrayal." The therapist was trying to replace the *either* sluttish *or* pure demonic dismantling with a *both* sluttish *and* loving antidemonic one. From Rachel's impish smile, he was glad to see that she did not reject the idea out of hand. Later she said that the memories served her as an aperitif, which prepared the palate for the meal.

The use of oxymorons like *positive exploitation* and *good betrayal* can be helpful in the antidemonic dialogue. In this case, Rachel showed herself an adept antidemonic "cook," by preparing herself a meal out of her memories of a sluttish past and her experience of a loving relationship. Rachel's cooking metaphor reflects, to our minds, an antidemonic shift in her attitude.

This chapter has many examples of the assembling and dismantling of conceptual units. It is precisely because these activities are so common that we tend not to notice them. We invite the reader to actively look in what follows for both their demonic and antidemonic varieties, so as to sharpen his ability to identify them and use them.

ANTIDEMONIC QUESTIONS

The parents of violent children are often asked, "What lies behind the child's aggressive behavior?" This question conveys the demonic assumption that the child's behavior is the external manifestation of a hidden problem (the enemy within) that must be exposed and eradicated. A different question, "When does the child manage to act in a nonviolent way?" conveys the contrary assumption that the behavior depends on circumstances and does not necessarily reflect the presence of negative hidden forces. Such a use of antidemonic questions is illustrated by the following interchange.

CASE 6

Michelle, a middle-aged single parent, described her problem with her 17-year-old son. He would suddenly yell and curse at her, and make demands in a most offensive manner. The outbursts raised in her fears that he was mentally ill, perhaps suffering from a multiple personality disorder, or from an unconscious hatred against women (the enemy within). This, to her mind, might explain why he still did not have a girlfriend. The therapist asked a series of questions:

Therapist: Does this behavior occur with other women too?

Michelle: No. On the contrary, he is quite charming with my woman friends.

Therapist: Then the behavior is probably not the result of an underlying hatred for women. Does he always treat you like that?

Michelle: No. Sometimes he is very nice with me too.

Therapist: Perhaps this shows we are not dealing with a basic hatred toward you, but with a more localized problem. Was he always like that?

Michelle: No. Until the age of 14, he was much more cooperative.

Therapist: And what happened when he was 14?

Michelle: We moved to another town. A lot of things changed.

Therapist: Perhaps the situation today is the result of adaptation difficulties, rather than a permanent personality trait. What happens after the outburst?

Michelle: It can go on for a few days but then usually he is contrite and sometimes even apologizes.

Therapist: So he does not think he has the right to lash out like a tyrant. This indicates he has moral feelings and is painfully aware that he hurt you. Are there any special circumstances in which he usually lashes out?

The discussion led Michelle to identify some circumstances that were commonly linked to the outbursts. She raised the possibility that her son sometimes burst out when he felt she was trying to "engineer" him unawares. She said she was so afraid that a direct approach would lead to an outburst that she often preferred to influence him indirectly. This dialogue brought her relief and led to some partial solutions that improved the relationship.

METAPHORS

The demonic view relies strongly on inflammatory images and metaphors. Talk of poison, back-stabbing, or betrayal can lead to extreme reactions. Fortunately, antidemonic images can be found, so as to cool the seething passions, slow down the drive to inexorable action, and redirect the attention to gradual solutions. Metaphors that use everyday objects can be especially effective—maybe because in their factual solidness, they counteract the demonic tendency to ignore the manifest in favor of the hidden. One such factual metaphor is that of *the therapeutic bolt.* This metaphor was used by one of us in the treatment of chronic posttraumatic clients (Alon, 1985), so as to help them refocus their attention from the negative and the traumatic to the small but cumulative positive changes in their lives.

CASE 7

Gideon, who had been wounded and traumatized in his military service, constantly repeated the hopeless statements, "There is no chance I'll ever be well again!" "The injury is beyond help!" "Words cannot untwist my brain." His view of his problem was that the trauma was such a deeply rooted implant in his mind that no treatment could ever reach it. The therapist interrupted his litany by taking out of the drawer a big bolt stuck deep inside a nut. Time and the elements had turned bolt and nut into one heavy rusty hunk. The therapist asked Gideon, "How would you pull the nut and the bolt apart?" Gideon, who was a mechanic, had his attention attracted by the question. He turned the bolt in his hands, examined it from all sides, and said:

Gideon: First you have to soak it in an antirust fluid for 24 hours. Then you put it in a vise, grip the nut with a wrench and start turning very gently.

Therapist: Why gently?

Gideon: Turning it too hard might break the coils.

Therapist: And which stage would be the hardest?

Gideon: The beginning. The oil can't get all the way in and you need more force and more care to make the first turn.

Therapist: And then?

Gideon: Then, as the oil gradually seeps in, it gets easier. Do you want me to open the screw for you?

Therapist: No, thank you. I brought it out because I thought you are a little like that bolt. You were hospitalized. There were attempts at rehabilitation. You were out of the circle of daily life for a long time. Your skills at work, at home, with friends, are all rusty. They have to be oiled and melted apart gradually. It is a slow process built out of small steps. You need oil, you need a wrench, care, and patience. As you said, the beginning is the hardest part. You have to move gently but forcefully. But as it starts moving, it gets easier.

The bolt was mentioned again whenever Gideon would become self-defeating. At the end of a lengthy but positive therapy, Gideon told the therapist that the bolt had given him the nudge that had started the improvement. Some of the metaphor's impact lies in its triviality; talk of rust, oil, coils, wrenches, and vises is a far cry from the unfathomable depths of the traumatized mind. This "trivialization" is typical of many antidemonic metaphors.

MODIFYING DEMONIC APPRAISALS

Assessing the Problem

Often what brings people to therapy is not the "objective" problem in itself, but the negative meaning they attribute to it. The worse the attributed meaning, the deeper is the condition supposed to be underlying the problem. For instance, one of us treated a number of people with a similar complaint—uncontrollable crying. The first saw the crying as a natural reaction to her mother's death, but was troubled by the fact that the crying appeared in embarrassing circumstances. The second viewed her crying as an ominous sign that she was losing control of herself. The third viewed her crying as proof of her husband's incurable cruelty. The initial complaint was similar in these cases, but the attributed negative meanings were wholly different. Whereas in the first case, the crying was viewed as a circumstantial problem, in the last two it was made into a sign of deeply negative processes. An antidemonic dialogue that modified these attributions might therefore bring some relief even before the problem itself was treated.

CASE 7

Sara, a highly successful lawyer, was convinced by her husband to come to an evaluation session, in spite of her belief that her problem was untreatable. Following a head injury in an accident, she had lost control of her laughter and crying. A light joke could lead her to uncontrollable laughter, a sad comment to convulsive crying. She felt so bad that she drastically curtailed her work and even considered quitting her job and profession.

Sara: I am a direct person and I do not hide my opinions. Don't be hurt, but I don't believe psychotherapy can help me. I only came here to satisfy my husband. I understand my problem in depth. The source is organic; there is no psychological factor involved. The brain cannot be repaired. Any treatment you give me is like treating cancer with aspirin.

Therapist: You are right. In view of the medical facts, psychotherapy cannot cure your condition. But perhaps it could give you some relief.

Sara: (with contempt) Now you're going to suggest I learn to live with the problem.

Therapist: In order to answer I have to understand a few things. What do you do when you start crying?

Sara: I try to get over the crying.

Therapist: How successful are you?

Sara: Not very (Sara began to cry and tried desperately to bring the crying under control. She bent over, buried her head in her hands, and rubbed her face hard—to no avail).

Therapist: Is this what usually happens to you with other people?

Sara: Yes! I can't stand to be seen like this, especially by my clients.

Therapist: It seems that your intense efforts to stop your crying are only making it worse. It is just like with sleeplessness, the harder you try to fall asleep the further you get from sleeping.

Sara: What do you suggest, that I tell my clients I am messed up?

Therapist: I'm not sure that's a bad idea. They see you cry anyway, and trying to hide it only makes it worse.

Sara: If that's the therapy I don't want it. What other ideas do you have?

Therapist: If we could reduce the problem by 30%, would it be worth a try?

Sara: In my condition, even 10% would be worth the effort.

Therapist: I think 30% is a realistic goal. We will try to reduce 10% by stopping to try so hard and another 10% by relaxation techniques. Maybe we can try to reduce another 10% by experimenting with selected clients that you trust and are willing to let in on your problem.

Sara agreed to give it a try. The first two measures brought some relief. She also spoke with a few clients with whom she felt comfortable and was surprised that they treated her with consideration. At the end of the treatment, she said with satisfaction that a 30% improvement had surely been achieved. This partial improvement sufficed for banishing all her thoughts of a change of profession.

The antidemonic twist in this case was the refocusing of attention from the core problem (the enemy within) to the circumstantial accretions that aggravate it. Viewing the problem as a big snowball with a smaller inner core can help in the treatment of many condition; insomnia, for instance—the harder one tries to fall asleep, the more upset one gets. Insomniacs often have an all-or-nothing attitude toward their problem: "If I sleep tonight all will be well; if not, I will be a total wreck." The antidemonic goal in such situations is to release the sufferer from this totalist frame of mind. In a few cases, we found it helpful to give the following message to clients with insomnia:

> Unfortunately we cannot solve your sleep problem directly. But the problem now is like a huge snowball that perhaps began with a stone that in rolling down the mountain carried with it snow, stones, twigs, and mud. Your struggle to fall asleep and your fear of the consequences are part of this growing snowball. We can reduce the snowball, but the stone inside it may remain. One of the problems with insomnia is that it deprives the body of rest. But there are other forms of rest—deep relaxation, for instance. So perhaps rather than trying to give insomnia a knock-out blow, we might look for some more effective way to rest. I can teach you relaxation. If this leads to sleeping—good. If not, you will at least get some rest.

Appraisal of Self

The demonic assessment leads to a sweeping condemnation of self or other. The guilt is not viewed as stemming from any specific faulty actions but as emanating from an inner essence or from the whole personality. No room is left for extenuating circumstances. This severe verdict comes from applying a strict "judgment by results." According to this principle, the negative results of an action are proof of the person's guilt. An even more demonic interpretation is that the negative results of an action reveal the person's "real" intentions. Thus miscarriages were viewed by some therapists as proof that the woman did not really want the baby, and premature ejaculation as proof that the man really wanted to frustrate the woman. Similarly, New Age adepts often say that "Something in you wanted the cancer" or that "She brought the disease upon herself." Disregard of circumstances is especially obvious in self-demonization. Thus, many clients blame their self-destructive tendency, when they fail to achieve a result such as a salary raise, a promotion, or a relationship with a wanted partner. For instance, a painting teacher reported that recently, the number of people applying for her courses had dropped sharply. She thought she was at fault for the drop because she "radiated a lack of drive." She dismissively waived the therapist's mention of the possible role of the economic crisis in the slowdown. She only began considering the circumstances when the therapist said that, although he did not suffer from lack of drive, he also had experienced a drop in referrals.

To modify the client's self-condemning stance, the therapist should acknowledge the problem's seriousness (without which the client would feel slighted or misunderstood), while contesting the severe verdict that the client passes on herself. In this respect therapists can learn from court procedures; the court always considers circumstances in weighing its verdict and its sentence.

CASE 8

Dina was a young dance student who was invited by an admired teacher to study privately with him. He complimented her on her talent and said he would make her into a great dancer. The flattering remarks were followed by seductive offers that gradually degenerated into a blatant and aggressive sexuality. Dina was afraid to put a stop to the abuse out of fear that the teacher would take revenge on her. She sunk into a depression. After a long time, she got the nerve to end the relationship but the depression did not go away. She viewed what had happened to her with the teacher as evidence of her lack of spine and moral masochism.

Therapist: And what do you think of your teacher's part?

Dina: I have nothing to say about him. He found a wimp and used her. It's my fault.

Therapist: My opinion is different. If any one is to blame here, it is not you but your teacher. What he did is nothing if not sexual exploitation of his status. By the way, that's a crime. If you charged him with it, even now, he might go to jail.

Dina: But I agreed.

Therapist: He took advantage of his position and power to abuse you.

Dina: I was the one who enabled him. I should have seen things for what they were and walked out!

Therapist: Not an easy task, in the state of mind you were in. At first you were flattered and enchanted by the way he treated you, right?

Dina: Right.

Therapist: You were 20 and inexperienced with men. You thought he was the perfect teacher. You believed him. The seduction proceeded in unnoticeable steps. First it was just coffee, then just visiting his studio, then just stage photos, then just nude photographs. No step in itself seemed awful. Seduction may only look like seduction in retrospect.

By highlighting the extenuating circumstances, the therapist gradually helped Dina view herself in a more forgiving light. Her depression began to clear. The reader might perhaps wonder whether Dina's acquittal was bought at the price of the teacher's demonization. Demonization involves not only a critical view of the other's acts, but also negative attributions of intent, the assumption of deep-lying negative characteristics, a view of these characteristics as deceptive and manipulatory, an interpretive lore that purports to unmask the deceit, a refusal of "superficial" compromises and a demand for radical solutions. Many of these are absent in the therapist's critical attitude toward the dance teacher.

In self-demonization, the sufferer is often prosecutor, inquisitor, judge, and executioner in one. The court procedure is a helpful metaphor because it keeps these roles strictly apart. For this reason, the institution of a therapeutic trial might enable an antidemonic reevaluation of the self.[3]

CASE 9

Samuel was a mechanic in the army tank corps. While his team was fixing a vehicle, Samuel was called to the phone. He left the garage and when he came back, he found out that the vehicle had fallen off the lift device and crushed a coremate to death. Samuel felt "he was the one who should have died." His reaction got worse when he was called to testify to the commission of inquiry that was examining the disaster; his guilt feelings caused

[3]Therapeutic trials have been occasionally mentioned in the literature (e.g., Greenberg & Witztum, 2001). We have given a detailed example in our book (Omer & Alon, 1997; pp. 160–169).

him to blame himself in front of the committee and avoid reporting serious safety lapses for which his superiors were responsible. A short time after the accident, Samuel was diagnosed as suffering from posttraumatic stress disorder and was discharged from reserve service. His situation worsened to the point of partial paralysis of the legs without an identified physical cause and he developed a severe stutter. Nightmares and scary visions by day deprived him of all rest. He refused psychological treatment but was partly helped by the sensitive care of his family doctor. This physician approached one of us with a request to try new therapeutic directions. Although Samuel did not want any psychotherapy, he agreed to a consultation because of his doctor's insistence. During the session, he would occasionally stare straight ahead at the empty space and look with horror at the ghost of the dead man, coming at him with his arms stretched forward to pull out his eyes. He was crushed by guilt and refused to consider any extenuating circumstances.

In a discussion with the doctor and with a professional colleague, the idea of a therapeutic trial came to mind. Because Samuel's putative crime had taken place in the army, it would befit the trial to take place in the army as well. But who in the army would want to get involved in this? The doctor and the therapist thought of a common friend, a high-ranking commander, who was a physician by training. The two went to him and explained that for a "therapeutic trial" they needed a general with a general's office and a general's manners, but an understanding heart. The friend agreed right away, and from there on the three acted as a therapeutic team. The doctor would take on the role of defense attorney, the therapist would be the prosecutor, and the officer would be the judge.

In the doctor's supportive presence, the therapist told Samuel his guilt feelings had a real basis; a life had been lost, and vital information had been concealed from the investigators, preventing remedial conclusions from being drawn. It is true that several years had gone by since the event, but now a senior officer had been found who was ready to get to the truth of the matter and bring it to the appropriate authorities. If Samuel were willing to fulfill his civic duty and testify in front of a senior officer, a corps commander, he would be given the chance to do so.

Samuel was shocked, but also attracted to the idea. He deliberated for a few days and finally agreed. Early on the day of the trial, Samuel and his wife arrived at the gate of the large base. A military car was waiting for Samuel at the entrance with a special entry permit for both of them. They were taken to the office of the corps commander, where the therapeutic team was already waiting. The bureau secretaries took them into the large conference room that was decorated with flags, banners, and maps.

Samuel entered solemnly and stood in front of the officer at the end of the conference table. He was wearing a suit and holding the cane that helped him with his limp.

The commander addressed Samuel without an introduction: "I heard from my friends that you were involved in a serious accident that was not sufficiently investigated. I am ready to complete the investigation, to try to understand what happened, to form an opinion, and to convey the findings to the appropriate authorities. Are you willing to cooperate?" Samuel answered in the affirmative. He told the whole story. The officer wrote down his words with a sealed expression. He asked many technical and practical questions, without addressing the emotional side or expressing sympathy. It was particularly important for him to understand why Samuel had chosen not to give full testimony to the investigators. There were moments when the therapist and the doctor thought the judge was being too strict. The investigation lasted a long time. When a technical question came up, Samuel suggested going to the military garage where the accident had occurred: "I can show you close up." On the ride and at the garage Samuel was under great stress. He breathed heavily and occasionally placed his hand on his chest. The therapist was glad there were two doctors at hand. It is not easy for a "criminal" to return to the scene of the crime. Luck helped, and Samuel was surprised to discover that some of his old coremates were at the garage! His friends were happy to see him, and his feeling that they must be angry at him dissipated. He was invited to another meeting to summarize the inquiry.

At this meeting, Samuel looked like a defendant before his death verdict. The commander summarized the main points of the inquiry at length, and then concluded:

> This inquiry addressed two points: the accident itself and the testimony to the committee. As for the accident, I find you not guilty. An accumulation of safety lapses along with a technical failure caused the accident. It is natural in such situations to feel as if you should have died instead of your friend, but that is just a feeling. You could not have prevented the death. When you were called to the phone, you did not know the disaster was going to happen. If you had known, you would have acted differently.

Samuel had heard similar words many times, but this time he heard them differently; after all, they were coming from a senior officer following a thorough inquiry.

> As for the testimony—you did fail. Even if you could not have brought your friend back, you could have helped expose the truth, expose those responsible and prevent similar disasters. But what motivated you was

> the feeling that you were the main guilty party and the difficulty of betraying your commanders. These are not negative motives. Yet you could have acted differently and the way you acted was wrong.
>
> On the other hand, you were willing, many years after the event, to disclose the whole truth. You were willing to come here, to open the old wounds, to risk a difficult inquiry; you were willing to suffer for the truth to come out. You deliberated at length until you made up your mind, and the decision required a lot of courage. The inquiry itself was difficult for you, yet you were willing to withstand it. The courage that you showed in this testimony offsets your lapse in the previous inquiry. [Samuel showed signs of major relief]. I will submit my conclusions to the army's tank corps for it to draw the necessary lessons. This late testimony erases the mistakes of the past and I find that you are no longer guilty and I thank you for the courage you displayed.

The commander parted with Samuel friendly. Samuel left the office with a lighter step. It was his last meeting with the therapist; he told the doctor he no longer wanted to see him. But he stayed in touch with the doctor, and through her, the case could be followed. The "trial" was followed by an enduring relief. A short time after the trial, Samuel was invited on a family vacation; since the accident, he had rejected all such offers, but he now agreed. From then on, he occasionally went on vacations and enjoyed them. He went back to his profession as a metalworker and he contributed an artistic rail to his dead friend's synagogue. His sleep improved and his scary visions diminished. He went over from the struggle for survival to the struggle for a better quality of life.

Learning to See Progress

Pain engages the sufferer's full attention. The person in pain has difficulty in noticing small improvements because the pain overshadows them. The demonic view adds another dark layer by disqualifying local improvements as irrelevant to the assumed deep processes. Thus, even in the face of an obvious improvement, the client may insist that "everything is the same." Therapists who are frustrated by such a client may at times react in an equally demonic spirit by concluding that "the client does not *want* to see the change." For these reasons, learning to notice and appreciate partial improvements is a vital element for both client and therapist.

CASE 10

Guy came to therapy with a feeling that his life was stuck. His university studies were in danger because he was unable to submit his papers on time. When he failed to pass his driving test for the third time, he decided he did not have the needed skills and decided not to try again. He was terrified of failure, and because to him every mistake was a failure, he opted for avoidance. He avoided girls, sports, papers, and now, driving lessons.

Guy was very impressed that his therapist engaged in the sport of paragliding. He had dreamt of engaging in this sport, but the dream seemed totally out of reach for him, for he "had neither guts nor talent." The therapist encouraged him to join a training school for paragliding, and to use the experiences in the training as material for the therapy. During the sessions, they would jointly examine how he reacted to his mistakes, failures, and partial successes. Guy's progress was indeed slower than that of most of the group, but he did make progress. Even though he enjoyed the course, he thought there was no point in continuing because "he had no talent," and "made mistakes all the time." His trainer urged him to continue. At the end of the course, all his colleagues got certified, whereas Guy was required to fly a few more times with supervision to improve his skill. He took this very badly and went into a depression that lasted for weeks. He told the therapist that "it had all been a waste of time." The therapist told him he wanted to see Guy's mistakes with his own eyes. It took some persuasion, but Guy agreed and the two took a paraglider and went to the beach. Taking off with a paraglider is a complex activity; one has to hold the strings correctly, run forward and wave the lines up, help the paraglider open up and balance it. The therapist proposed to divide this complex activity into small units. He told Guy: "Now pay attention only to the running. I don't care what happens to your hands or to the paraglider; only the running matters." Guy ran well and the paraglider started rising. Guy's face was gloomy.

Guy: It wasn't good.

Therapist: Why?

Guy: Because I did not wave the strings.

Therapist: I told you that we begin only with the running, not with the other things.

Guy: (critically) You think I can't think about two things at the same time!

On the therapist's urging, he agreed to repeat the run and leave the other details alone. The next step was to run and wave the strings. The therapist stressed that what mattered now was the combination of running and waving the hands. The therapist specifically said that for the moment it did not matter if the paraglider went up a little and fell away right afterward. Guy followed the instructions satisfactorily.

Guy: Shit!

Therapist: Why?

Guy: The paraglider didn't stay up.

Therapist: I didn't ask for it to stay up.

Guy: I get it. You don't believe I can do it, right? Let's stop, this isn't going to work.

The therapist insisted and Guy agreed again. Even when Guy succeeded in getting the paraglider up for the whole run, he remained disappointed, saying that he had only succeeded because the therapist had guided him step by step. The therapist concluded: "The last two hours have taught me more about your difficulties than the whole therapy. In our talks, you told me how you avoid things and get depressed, but today you showed how this happens. I think we can now study the mechanism together in detail." The next therapy hours were devoted to studying Guy's tendency to bemoan his mistakes instead of learning from them. Potentially useful mistakes thus went to waste. Guy agreed that his self-flagellation, his fear of mistakes, and his avoidance were deeply damaging. The paragliding became a helpful example for understanding and reducing Guy's self-disqualifying processes and his ensuing paralysis.

The reader might wonder, "Why did the therapist take a problem of negative self-image and reduce it to a series of trivial mistakes in running and hand-waving? Had the therapist abandoned psychology and started a new career as a sports trainer?"

The impression of trivialization is not farfetched. In the antidemonic dialogue, major problems are often broken down into a number of small but expanding processes. As in the snowball metaphor, the work of peeling off the accumulating dirt deals with "superficials," but it can help in reducing the snowball to tolerable proportions. In this kind of dialogue, the client is not given the blame for not seeing the change, nor is he or she assumed to be in a power struggle with the therapist. Seeing the changeable positive is not easy when one is used to focusing on the constant negative.

CASE 11

Anna's husband, Dave, was in the habit of exploding over minor occurrences, threatening he would leave home if things went on as they were. Anna lived in fear of him. Sometimes she thought the threats were serious, but at other times she thought Dave used them only to intimidate her, so as to make himself strong and superior. Usually, she would cower in silence, wait for the storm to pass, and then approach him with tearful apologies (she called this "crawling and begging"). Dave would sharply criticize her, but after awhile, both would go back to a more normal routine, until the next outburst. Anna was sure she could not act differently; she felt she could not live without knowing for sure that Dave was no longer furious at her. The therapist and Anna decided to set up an experiment in which Anna would, for a limited time, make some systematic changes in her usual behavior in order to check her hypotheses about Dave's intentions and about her own possibilities of reacting. She was to make two changes: (a) skip the "crawling and begging" stage and start talking to Dave normally after the storm was over, and (b) talk to him about the negative effect his outbursts had on her. The logic of the experiment was as follows: If Dave really wanted to keep her down and prove he was strong and superior, he would try to browbeat Anna into going back to the "crawling and begging stance," would prolong his biting criticisms, and would react angrily to Anna's mention of the negative effect his outbursts had on her. The experiment would also put to the test Anna's own ability to react differently.

Anna: I did what we agreed and it didn't help at all.

Therapist: What was his reaction to what you did?

Anna: Again he got mad and started threatening. He simply won't change.

Therapist: And how did you respond? Was your response the same as usual?

Anna: (thinking) Not exactly. This time I didn't cry or apologize. Somehow I wasn't so scared of his anger.

Therapist: Do you consider that a change?

Anna: (hesitant) Yes. And the fact that I wasn't afraid felt good.

Therapist: What happened after the outburst?

Anna: We didn't speak for 3 days.

Therapist: And how did that end?

Anna: I started talking to him as if nothing happened.

Therapist: Did he go back to criticizing you?

Anna: No. He too reacted as if nothing happened.

Therapist: That is a change. Usually you go through the "crawling and begging" moves and he explains how wrong you were.

Anna: Right.

Therapist: After you made up did you talk to him about the bad effect his outbursts have on you?

Anna: Yes. It was hard for me because I am so used to smoothing things over to maintain peace.

Therapist: And how did he respond?

Anna: He listened quietly and then added, "It's no big deal."

Therapist: Is that a change?

Anna: Maybe. I was surprised he didn't get angry again. (Laughing) you are asking quite a lot from me— to make changes and notice them, too.

This work of "noticing the changes" had to be repeated a few times, and Anna became gradually more proficient at this task. Although Dave's outbursts did not vanish, Anna's fear and humiliation diminished considerably.

NONDEMONIC GOALS

In the demonic view, cure can only be achieved by eliminating the deep-lying cause of the suffering. Nondemonic goals, in contrast, are small and partial. These goals may initially disappoint the client, particularly if he or she believes in the need for root treatment. Such a gap requires negotiation.

Let us go back to Ralph, the client who felt he could not change until his mother gave him back the love she had not given him when he was a child (see chapter 2).

Ralph: As long as I keep running into my mother's lies, I can't get out of my depression. She has to see things the way they are!

Therapist: I am afraid that is something I cannot help you with.

Ralph: Why?

Therapist: You have tried to change your mother's attitude for many years. You failed. I don't think I can do any better than you did.

Ralph: So how can you help me? Could you at least help me not care about the way I was treated?

Therapist: Only completely impervious people can stay indifferent to a difficult past. But we might perhaps achieve a more modest goal. Today you feel so overwhelmed by the past that you avoid doing things that would help you feel better, such as socializing. Perhaps by engaging in some of the avoided activities, the shadow of the past would diminish.

Ralph agreed to this proposal. In this way, the very process of negotiating over the therapeutic goals may get the antidemonic process underway.

CASE 12

Sean, a young student, tormented himself about the harm he had caused to another child whom he had bullied years before. He felt what he had done was unforgivable, that it pointed to a deep moral flaw in his character, and that he had to suffer to atone for his sins. The self-mortification, however, proved ineffective, for he never felt he had suffered enough.

The therapist told him about the distinction Tibetan Buddhists make between "guilt" and "remorse." *Guilt* is a feeling directed at the past: "How awful is what I did and what a horrible human being I am!" *Remorse* is directed at the future: "How can I avoid stumbling again and how can I add some good to the world to somewhat compensate for the evil I caused?" Guilt, the Tibetans say, has value only when it leads to remorse; if not, it is a waste of time. Sean described his wish for complete atonement by quoting the prophet, Isaiah: "Though your sins be scarlet, they shall be as white as snow." The therapist commented: "That may be true at the end of days. Meanwhile, we have to be satisfied with 'Though your sins be scarlet, they shall become off-white.' There are stains that do not come out completely in the wash, but they can be lightened." The therapist suggested they should work for a change from "past-oriented guilt" to "future-oriented remorse." Once Sean accepted the idea of a partial improvement, he became able to undertake positive actions that proved beneficial for others and himself.

"It is stronger than me!" "It takes control of my actions!" "I cannot withstand it!" says the alcoholic, the explosive parent, the battering man, or the sexual exhibitionist. On occasion, most people think in similar terms about their own slips. This belief in a negative force that resides deep in the soul and gains control over it received a pseudoscientific varnish with the spread of pop psychology. A major representative of this putative negative force is the repressed trauma. In this view, the traumatic condition can only be cured if the trauma is fully brought to consciousness and undergoes a process of abreaction. As we argued in chapter 2, this procedure can be viewed as a kind of secular exorcism. Classical movies, such as Hitchcock's *Marnie* or Redford's *Ordinary People*, in which both the mystery and the suffering are resolved as the trauma is relived and discharged, have given these ideas a high popular standing.

These therapeutic procedures have been subjected to a triple criticism in the last years: (a) the study of memory has shown there is no way to establish what is real and what is imagined when putative memories are thus brought to consciousness, (b) the negative meaning the person attaches to the events may cause no less misery than the events themselves, and (c) revival of a negative experience may intensify its impact rather than diminishing it.

These criticisms question the need and the value of reaching for the "real" trauma in the treatment of posttraumatic clients. An alternative goal could be the more modest one of reducing the client's acute reactions in the present. The therapist might say to the traumatized client,

> Perhaps your suffering does not stem so much from the underlying trauma, but from the fact that your feelings today are keenly aroused by anything that reminds you of it. You then react in mind and body as if you were about to have the traumatic experience all over again. If these automatic responses could be reduced, you would not suffer so much.

CASE 13

Will, who had been wounded years ago in a terrorist attack, needed a critical eye surgery but refused to have it. He was hospitalized for the surgery but during the preparations, he was flooded by memories of the hospital in which he had been treated with the other victims of the attack. He ripped off the instruments and ran out of the operating room. He refused to return and said he would rather lose his eyesight than go back and revisit that experience. The present therapist proposed to help Will to disconnect the new hospital, in which he should undergo his eye surgery, from the emotional reactions linked to the terrorist attack. Will only agreed when he was reassured that no attempt would be made to have him reexperience the original trauma. The therapist helped Will enter deep relaxation and to imagine he was holding the remote control of a VCR in his hands:

> Take the remote control in your hand ... turn on the set ... change the show to black and white ... bring back the color ... make it pinker... make it run quickly like in old movies ... add music that does not match the plot. If the movie has uncomfortable parts you do not want to watch, turn it off. Now put in the film with the sticker that says, "Will's eye operation." The movie begins and you see the waiting room of the hospital's eye department. Now, as you see yourself in the eye department, imagine there is a VCR there, in which you can see another movie, a film within the film, which is called "Will's terrorist experience." In it you can see the hospital where you and the other victims were treated, but all along you know you are in the eye department and you know you came for an operation that will save your eyesight. The hospital with the terror victims looks far away, hazy ... you see the wounded Will laying on a stretcher ... but you are here, in the eye department, and you can watch Will from a distance in the terrorism movie. The terrorism movie continues ... you can see yourself getting wounded ... being evacuated ... being hospitalized ... but this time not "from the inside," through your eyes, but from the outside, as it appears in the film. You can dull the movie, reduce the volume, or turn it off, because you have the remote control in your hand. You know that the Will in the film is afraid to die, but you don't have to feel that fear

> now, for you know what the wounded Will does not know—that he is going to survive ... and therefore you can see the film with far less fear ... now, in the eye department, knowing also that there is a good chance the treatment will remove the part of your difficulties that can be removed, leaving only a smaller part that cannot be removed, because you went through really difficult things.

The readiness of the therapist to settle for less enabled him to present a modest and acceptable goal to the client. This partial approach allowed Will, after a treatment that lasted a few hours, to get through the eye operation.

REDUCING DEMONIC ZEAL

The demonic view entails a compelling need for immediate and decisive action, for any postponement or hesitation could only make things worse. For example, a young woman says to a boyfriend who did not call as promised: "Tell me now, do you want to be with me or not? If not, let's stop right now!" Or, a worker says to his boss after the boss expressed discontent with his work: "I see you don't need me anymore. So I quit!" On this view, decisive action is all. Anything less would be groveling.

It is commonly held that doubt is the opposite of action. Hamlet and the obsessive client are paralyzed by their endless deliberations. Great actions, however, may also issue from a determination not to act prematurely and patiently to endure a state of indecision. Toronaga, the hero of Clavell's *Shogun*, illustrates this kind of active waiting. Toronaga stood at the head of a camp threatened by a superior enemy, was surrounded by generals who called for daring action, and was ridiculed for his lack of fiber. Withstanding all pressure to act prematurely, he followed closely the developments within and without his camp. He understood that he could not, in an act of will, cut through the knot of political and military forces. All he could do was hitch his efforts to the existing forces, adding perhaps a critical weight that, at the right moment, might make a shift in the balance. This attitude, which we would term *the ripening principle*, involves:

1. Avoiding the illusion of a knock-out blow or a once-and-for-all solution.
2. Accepting that many factors are involved and that one's influence is perforce limited.
3. Watching for the opportune moment when decisive action can shift the balance in a desired direction.

The ripening principle counters the demonic combination of polarized thinking and militant zeal that is expressed in sayings like: "It's now or never!" or "Attack or surrender!" Viewed through the lens of the ripening principle, the two poles in these sayings lose their absolute and exclusive significance. Far from signifying the pale cowardliness and spineless shilly-shallying that the demonic perspective makes of it, the ripening principle may involve a revolutionary attitude. This can be seen from the following examples.

Active Waiting

Extramarital relationships often cause enormous suffering for the whole family. When an affair is disclosed, fierce emotions with a high destructive potential arise. A demonizing attitude toward the self ("There is something about me that makes men leave me!"), the betrayer ("He is a sex maniac!"), or the relationship ("This proves our marriage was diseased!") may add another layer to the feelings of loss and anger. Such demonic descriptions lead to escalation, invalidate all positive elements, and make dialogue impossible. The betrayed party turns to friends and relatives for help, but often gets contradictory advice: "Tell him bluntly: It is her or me!" or "Lie low and don't wreck your marriage!" The ripening principle offers an unconventional alternative.

CASE 14

Ida, who had been in therapy with her husband, Simon, in the past, asked for an urgent appointment. She had discovered in Simon's credit card report payments for expensive restaurants and fancy hotels. From a conversation with the secretaries in his law office, she learned that Simon and Shelly, a young lawyer, had traveled together to court hearings out of town. Her friends advised Ida to "throw him out of the house." Ida said that anything less than a peremptory, "It's either her or me!" would make her feel like a doormat. On the other hand, she felt extremely afraid of the consequences of such an ultimatum. This dilemma brought her to therapy again.

Ida was a talented and successful fashion designer. She had first come to therapy because of anxiety states that led her to become more and more dependent on Simon's continuous support. In the beginning, he was willing to help but gradually became more and more averse to Ida's endless phone calls. He became distant and immersed himself in work. Ida had then felt threatened both in her marriage and in her personal and professional independence. The therapy, partly individual and partly marital, helped her regain her self-reliance.

This time, Ida was beset with doubts: "What is wrong with our marriage? How come I believed he loved me? What made me so blind? Was I a sucker?

Is he basically a liar?" She found herself wavering between vilifying Simon, herself, and the marriage.

Therapist: What kind of help do you want?

Ida: I want to feel strong.

Therapist: Strong to do what?

Ida: He has to decide. He has to choose between her and me.

Therapist: What steps do you think you have to take?

Ida: My friends are right. I have to tell him I know, show him my proof, and tell him he has to choose. But I am weak. I am afraid he will decide to go and build a new life with her or with another woman. That would shatter me. I know he will start arguing over the evidence, and I will give way.

Therapist: How do you understand what happened?

Ida: Maybe he felt threatened by my independence. He would prefer a woman who is insecure and obedient, who would revere him blindly, and feed his ego. At his age, he also needs proof of his masculinity. So in comes Shelly!

Therapist: Have you felt any changes in his attitude toward you or the family lately?

Ida: Not at all. But he was under a lot of stress lately and I thought it was because he was having a crisis at work. But now I think the reason might be different. Maybe he was planning to discard me all along!

Therapist: Would such a scheming strategy suit his style?

Ida: If you asked me before this summer I would have said no. He used to be sincere and say what he thought. But it turns out I was wrong. He seems to be much more devious than I had ever thought possible.

Therapist: I want to help you find power, but I am not sure the right way is to make an ultimatum.

Ida: What do you mean?

Therapist: If you are right, and he went out with this woman because your relationship is rotten or because he is just a plain bastard, then what you want to do makes sense; that sort of problem should be handled by a direct attack. But the question is whether those descriptions fit his motives.

Ida: I don't understand.

Therapist: Common wisdom is that an extramarital relationship indicates a deep problem in the marriage or a basic personality flaw. But I am not sure it is so.

Ida: What else could it be?

Therapist: Sometimes one gets into an affair by small steps, none of which looks very dangerous in itself: "We are just going to have a cup of coffee together;" "We are just going to look at the sea." There is usually an illusion of control: "We will have sex just once and then stop." Slowly, things get entangled and what might have looked small at the beginning is now a huge affair. When you began smoking at 16, did you tell yourself you were becoming an addict? No! You told yourself you just want to try, to see what smoking is like, to check your control. The nature of seduction is that each step in itself is not experienced as seduction. I don't know if this is what happened to Simon. But it could be. As I remember him, I don't think a frontal attack would be a good idea. It would probably escalate the situation and deepen the rift.

Ida: Okay, let's say for a moment that he was tempted and there is no deep problem in our relationship. What would be the right thing to do then?

Therapist: I would propose a line of action that may seem strange at first, but that I tried successfully in a few cases. This line would put demands on you, but would increase the chances of overcoming the affair and the crisis.

Ida: I am not sure I want to stay in a failed marriage.

Therapist: If it failed and you decide you don't want it—I am willing to help you end it in the right way. This line will actually strengthen you also for that option. But I just think you shouldn't get rid of the marriage before it is sure that the marriage is a failure.

Ida: Do you want to tell me I have to pretend and lie low until he is tired of screwing his assistant?

Therapist: I want to suggest a line that is neither cringing nor aggressive. The advantages of this line are that it does not wreck the relationship and that it opens the chance for new developments. The hard part is that it requires you to stay undecided for awhile, whereas you want certainty and decision now. I propose you ask Simon for a talk, and tell him:

> I know you are having an affair with Shelly. I know it for sure, out of female intuition. You don't need to answer, confirm, or deny what I am saying. I am not asking you if it's true, I don't need to prove it's true, whatever you say won't change my certainty. Don't ask me for proof—I don't need anything beyond my certainty. It's extremely painful for me to think of your choosing to be with another woman. It hurts me deeply as a woman. But that is my problem and I can deal with it. I also believe that our relationship is deep and strong. If I am right, it will withstand this crisis. And if it doesn't, I'll understand it was not good and strong

> enough, and then I'll be able to end it. I know that I am deeply attached to you. Even though I am awfully hurt and angry, what I feel for you after 25 years will not be erased. I am not asking you for anything. I am not telling you how to act towards her, I am not demanding you to choose or decide right now. Emotionally I would like to tell you to throw her out and fire her from the office, but I want you to make your own decision. I believe that if you understand my feelings, you will know what to do, but you are free to act as you understand. I am responsible for handling my pain. I have patience. One day I may decide to make an end of my uncertainty, but now I am choosing only one thing: to let you know, to take care of myself, and to hope you understand.

Ida: No way! He will see this as permission to go even further and throw all consideration overboard.

Therapist: If that happens, that will be clear proof that he is a schmuck and I will help you fight your way out of the marriage. In a sense we are making a scientific experiment: If his behavior toward you improves and you see signs he is in a real dilemma, then our line is justified. If he goes on flouting his affair before you even more openly, then he is no partner, and our experiment helped us reach a greater readiness for the fight ahead.

Ida: You make it sound so easy. This crazy idea somehow fits my wishes, but I don't know if I can handle it. I'd have to consult with you frequently. It's so easy to siip.

Therapist: I'll be available to you online. We can talk on the phone or meet as frequently as you see fit.

The therapist met Ida again the next day, and she told him of her talk with Simon:

> He tried to deny, but I told him there was no point. He demanded to know on what basis I was accusing him. I told him that as a lawyer he would always be better than me at evidence, but that my intuition sufficed for me. He tried to attack, but I managed not to be drawn into an argument. But when he stormed out of the room, I felt terrible. During the night he told me he was feeling very bad. He feared he was having a heart attack. I could not resist saying he deserved one. But then I helped him to calm down.

In the following days, the therapist met often with Ida. He helped her stick to the chosen line despite the anger and fear she felt intermittently. Simon began to get closer to her, called her frequently, worried about her, and invited her out.

Ida: He hasn't cared about me so much for a long time. But I feel it all comes from guilt and not from real feeling.

Therapist: Well, bastards don't usually feel guilt.

Ida asked her friends to help her without telling her what to do. She thus reduced the external pressure to reach a decision. Simon continued to woo her and to feel bad. One day he called the therapist and asked for an appointment. He came with Ida but asked to speak to the therapist alone with Ida's agreement.

Simon: You must have heard from Ida about Shelly. I was blindly drawn into an affair with her. I didn't mean it but I got carried away. Shelly is a vulnerable and hot-tempered woman and I was afraid to cut off the relationship. The affair made me neglect my work to the point that some major clients left me. Ida found out about it. In the confrontations we had, I discovered she was stronger than I ever thought possible. She handled this crisis fantastically. I saw it broke her heart, but she kept cool. I was in a terrible conflict and started feeling ill. I never confirmed her suspicions nor denied them. She didn't press me in either direction. Suddenly I realized how important she is to me. I decided to break off with Shelly. The day before yesterday I told Shelly I had decided to break up. She looked at me with a wild look and said, "Really? You think you can just dump me? I'll show you. I am calling Ida now!" And she picked up the phone. I heard her call Ida and say, "This is Shelly. Your husband promised to marry me and now he is dumping me! I want you to know I'll never give him up!" She burst out crying and continued talking to Ida. I didn't hear what Ida said. When they stopped talking, Shelly looked at me with hatred and said, "Ida is on her way over here!" I was shocked. I waited for the ceiling to fall on me. Ida came in. She looked beautiful, elegant, and calm. She completely ignored me, went over to Shelly and said to her with warmth, "How could you have believed his promises? He always gets carried away. I am sure he didn't mean to leave home." Then she turned to me and said, "How could you fool this young woman? Don't you have any scruples?" And to Shelly: "Let's go to the other room. Tell me everything." I was shocked. I didn't know where to bury myself. They shut themselves in the other room. I heard Shelly crying and Ida comforting her. They came out of the other room. Shelly came up to me, slapped me on the face and said, "You'll see! You'll pay for what you did to me!" I staggered and went to the door.

At this point in Simon's story, the therapist could not control himself and started laughing. Simon started laughing too, though a little sourly. No soap opera could stage a situation like that. Simon went on:

> Ida sat at the table and said calmly, "Why are you running away? Stay and take it like a man!" And then Shelly said, "I always thought you were an angel and Ida was a monster. Now I see it's exactly the other way around. You can't even appreciate the wife you have. You bastard!" And she stomped out. Ida and I stayed alone. I felt very close to her, and somehow started to tell her that the crisis at the office had been linked to my bad condition since the start of the affair. That was the reason I was about to lose the firm that had always been my best client. I confided in her. I felt she was far stronger then me. She wanted me to call the firm's president right away. I told her I was too embarrassed. She knew him well because we had worked for so long together and the families had met a few times, so she asked me for his cell phone number and called him. She told him, "I understand you want to stop working with Simon. The whole time I thought it was you who was out of line, but today I understood why he neglected his commitments. I want to meet you to explain the situation to you." I heard him say over the speaker phone that if it were me calling, he would have hung up on me but because of her, he was willing to meet with us. He invited us to his house that very evening. Ida told him, "Simon was having an affair that got him into trouble and made him neglect his work. If you drop him, his office could collapse. For years he did a great deal for you. Your achievements as president were partly to his credit. What just happened was a passing matter. I am asking you to give him another chance and I guarantee he will make amends for his failings." He told us he was willing to give me a new chance.

Ida later told me the same story as Simon, but with one addition:

> When Shelly called me, I was crushed, because Simon had never officially admitted the affair. My first impulse was to lash out at her and make a scene. But then I remembered what we had talked about—not to attack and not to grovel. I decided to act in the most restrained manner possible. I don't know where I got the strength, but I never felt so much power as a woman. At the office I really enjoyed watching him squirm.

A follow-up a few years later showed that the crisis had been overcome and even led to an improvement in the relationship.

The Scientific Experiment

One way to implement the ripening principle is the aforementioned *scientific experiment.* In the previous case, Ida tested her hypotheses about the marital relationship by holding her wish for decisive action at bay, while experimentally modifying her usual behavior. The following case illustrates a very rapid experiment, showing that instant ripening is also possible.

CASE 15

Mika had had a driving license for 20 years but had been too anxious to drive. She had recently separated from her husband and now lived in a small town with her teenage children. The children were going to school in the nearby city and they needed to be driven. She felt the fact she did not drive made them view her as a sort of handicapped person and she was afraid that would undermine the children's trust in her. In the last years, she had tried to take driving lessons but she lacked the confidence to drive on her own. She attributed her fear of driving to an unconscious fear of independence. She said she had called the therapist to ask for hypnotherapy, because only deep hypnosis could help her get to the depth of her problem. The therapist told her on the phone that he was leaving for a lengthy trip abroad in one week. However, he agreed to meet her. The following dialogue took place in the first session:

Therapist: If the problem really stems from an unconscious fear of independence, you will need a deep and extensive treatment. In such case, I can refer you to a good therapist who does such work [Mika looked disappointed]. On the other hand, maybe the problem is more superficial and comes from the cumulative effects of long-term avoidance. It is in the nature of avoidance that it worsens the fear. In that case, we might be able to do a simple and quick therapy, and I am willing to try it in the 5 days before I leave.

Mika: How do we know what kind of problem it is?

Therapist: I suggest we do a scientific experiment to rule between the two alternatives.

Mika: What is the experiment?

Therapist: Today is Thursday. Buy a car tomorrow. Then we'll meet at your house and I'll help you practice driving. If the diagnosis is "avoidance," you'll be driving by the time I leave on Tuesday.

Mika: You're kidding.

Therapist: Buying a car is not complicated.

Mika: But I never bought a car.

Therapist: Take a friend with you who understands about such things.

Mika: And what if it turns out to be a deep problem and not an avoidance problem?

Therapist: Then you can sell the car and I'll give you the phone numbers of therapists that work with a deeper approach. If you choose to go on with the scientific experiment, call me tomorrow after you have the car.

Mika: But how will I get the car home from the city?

Therapist: That's a technical problem. Maybe the friend who helps you buy the car can drive you home.

On Friday afternoon, the therapist got a call: "The Fiat Uno is standing outside."

On Sunday, the therapist came to Mika's house. By the time he got there Mika had already had a few hours of driving on the internal roads, accompanied by a friend. They drove together around the town, and the therapist found that her driving, although far from smooth, was safe. They drove also on the main roads around the town. After the session Mika thought it unnecessary for the therapist to visit her again the next day. She has been driving since—except for the road to Jerusalem. They agreed that "Jerusalem was a deep problem," in all possible meanings.

This scientific experiment illustrates all the elements of the ripening principle. The client wanted hypnotherapy because of her assumption that some negative inner force was preventing her from driving. The therapist viewed her assumption as legitimate, but offered an alternative hypothesis and proposed an experiment to test the two views. The conditions of the experiment provided the ripening conditions that might lead to a change. Buying the car was of course not a neutral "scientific" act, but one that initiated the ripening processes; the car was no longer an abstract idea but a very concrete reality. Habits of paralyzing self-analysis were shortcut, and an element of surprise and humor was introduced into an area that was previously ruled by negative feelings. Besides, it is hard not to sit down in the driver's seat when you have a brand new car parked outside your house.

CASE 16: A MIXTURE OF ANTIDEMONIC THEMES

Eli was called to reserve military service at the end of the Lebanon War. He was in charge of operating special electronic equipment in a sealed underground room. He worked mostly alone and in long and monotonous shifts. In the third day of strenuous work on a task of the highest responsibility, Eli became flooded with anxiety. The equipment seemed not to be reacting as it should. The technical difficulties and the high anxiety brought him to a state in which he felt that the letters on the screen were taking the shape of scary faces. His commander was on sick leave, and returned to the unit the next day. Eli was sent to the infirmary, where he waited alone for another 7 hours before a physician examined him and decided to transfer him to a psychiatric hospital in the rear. Eli was hospitalized for 3 months, a period that he remembers as one of endless suffering. The medications caused him severe side-effects, and he felt his condition was worsening day by day. To cap it all off, the ward psychologist told him repeatedly that he would not get better unless he accepted that he was mentally ill. A change in the medications, however, led to an improvement that made his discharge from the hospital possible. Eight months later, Eli started a new job. His sense of responsibility led him to work long hours and to tax himself beyond his capacity. The stressful symptoms reappeared and he was plagued with frightening visions. A 2-month hospitalization followed, and Eli was discharged with a diagnosis of schizophrenia. The army discharged him from reserve duty on psychiatric grounds. Eli felt that the army had neglected him, and that his whole medical treatment had been a big mistake. He feared that people would come to know about his psychiatric discharge and therefore decided to keep a low profile. He avoided asking for a promotion and always backed down in situations of conflict. Nobody ever bothered to tell him of his rights as a disabled army veteran. Years went by before he made inquiries and found the courage to apply to the Ministry of Defense to be recognized as a military casualty.

One of the few positive things in his life was his relationship with his wife, Delia, whom he had met a few years after the hospitalization. Soon after meeting Delia, he decided to tell her everything about his past. Delia was not scared, agreed to marry him, and encouraged him to look for a better job and to strive to make the most of his professional capacity. Eli, however, was too intimidated, feeling constantly threatened by the shadow of his psychiatric past.

The therapist and Eli recognized a common element in the two crises. In both he had been overburdened, slept very little, smoked nonstop, drank countless cups of coffee, and hardly ate or drank, except for the coffee. The therapist remarked that the excessive nicotine, caffeine, and sleep deprivation had badly overtaxed his psychophysiological capacity. Eli said that he tended to load himself with coffee and cigarettes whenever he had to cope with a stressful situation at work. The therapist told Eli that he and Delia should keep this risk factor in mind for the future.

The reader is now invited to enter the therapist's shoes for a while. The session with Eli is about to end. It is, of course, too early to provide a comprehensive description of Eli's condition, to say nothing of a detailed therapeutic plan. Yet, an interim summary may be in order. Here are some possible antidemonic formulas for such a summary.

A Combination of Susceptibility and Circumstances (The Epoxy Glue Model)

There are two competing diagnoses about you: *schizophrenia,* as the hospital thinks, and *acute stress reaction,* as you think, without actually using the term. But perhaps what happened to you is neither schizophrenia nor an ordinary stress reaction, but an unlucky combination of susceptibility and circumstances. We saw you have a peculiar susceptibility to a constellation that involves overburdening, sleep deprivation, excessive coffee and cigarettes. Normally this susceptibility does not become manifest. But the extreme circumstances that led to your two hospitalizations were just of the kind to which you are most vulnerable. Without the susceptibility, the circumstances would probably not have affected you that way. Without the circumstances, the susceptibility would probably have remained dormant. The combination is what triggered the crisis. Your problem works somewhat like epoxy glue. This glue comes in two separate tubes, each with a fluid that has no adhesive quality. But when you mix the two, you get a really strong glue. The same may be true about you; in all probability you could have managed fine with each factor separately, but the combination was fatal.

The Snowball

When we look at things today we can see a huge life problem. But we can compare it to a snowball that gets formed around a slipping stone. The ball looks huge, but only its inner core is solid. Your initial problem was an acute crisis that undoubtedly had a psychotic element. But added to that crisis were the effects of hospitalization, such as social isolation, the development of a negative self-image, and a gradual disconnection from normal life and work. Later on, more snow stuck to the snowball: your fear of being unmasked, your tendency to avoid conflicts, your lurking fear that the condition might return. Even if we suppose that at the core of that snowball lies the stone that we term *psychosis,* and even if we assume that this susceptibility to psychosis is still there and cannot be changed, we can still remove big parts of the snowball and turn the problem from being "this big" (the therapist holds his hands far apart) to "this big" (the therapist holds his hands closer together).

The Last Straw

Perhaps what happened to you was a gradual accumulation of burdens, until one more straw was added that broke your back. I don't know all of the burdens in your life, but I suppose going to the army was a big one. Your regular job was a burden. The long service was a burden. The war was an even bigger burden. The high responsibility and your physical condition during the crisis were additional burdens. Every person has a point where even a little extra burden can lead to a crash.

Right Idea, But Wrong Application

You are a hard worker and you care very much about living up to your responsibility. That is how you acted for years and that policy served you well in your life. In your parents' home, you worked hard to be a model child. You studied hard and became an outstanding student. You worked hard at your military service and were appreciated. Wherever you worked you set yourself the highest standards and succeeded. It was natural that you should work very hard and be extremely responsible in your reserve army service as well. But you did not take into consideration that circumstances in the war were different, and that going all the way as you always did might lead to rapid burnout. "Going all the way" in the context of the service is different from "going all the way" as a university student. The idea was fine, but its application in these circumstances was wrong and that led to the crisis.

Bad Luck

I agree that your life got messed up, but I disagree with your interpretation. You feel with justice that you were badly treated by the system and that a whole series of errors was committed. However, I think there was an additional player in your drama—bad luck! This may not sound very scientific or psychological, but I think that luck is one of the forces that contribute to making a life. If circumstances were a little different, if your commander had not been sick that day, or if a friend had sent you to sleep for some hours, maybe the whole thing wouldn't have happened. The combination of bad luck coming from a lot of directions at once was fatal.

And what did the therapist actually say? He combined those formulas:

I think what happened to you at the hospital was the result of highly negative circumstances, a big mishap, and a misunderstanding with tragic results. The crisis was very acute and, unfortunately, you got the wrong treatment. This has dictated much of your history ever since.

I think what happened to you in the war should be viewed as a *combat reaction* and not as a *psychotic breakdown. Combat reaction* is any emotional reaction that emerges during combat service and as a reaction to it. Experience in all armies shows that the best treatment of combat reaction, whatever its form and severity, is a treatment that takes place very close to the front and to the time of the injury with a full expectation of returning as quickly as possible to fitness and service. The history of treatments for combat reaction shows that disconnecting a soldier from his military environment and treating him in a civilian hospital worsens the problem. Under these conditions, chances are that a graver diagnosis may come into effect, further stigmatizing the patient and limiting the chances of rehabilitation.

Unfortunately you served in a small unit without a medical support system. Your mates knew nothing about combat reactions. They were alarmed and did what seemed to them the most reasonable thing—they sent you to the infirmary and the psychiatrist transferred you to a hospital in the rear. When you got to the hospital, the snowball was already rolling, and the series of mistakes continued there. The civilian system operated the way it is used to, and you were put in a psychiatric ward. There was nobody there to identify the problem as combat reaction. The hospital was understaffed because of the war and there was nobody there who knew anything about the right treatment. The medications you received probably worsened your condition instead of improving it. The very length of the hospitalization aggravated the situation even more. These circumstances set the stage for much that came afterward.

The hospitalization made a deep break in your life. You began to see yourself as sick. You started to be afraid. You started to hide. The snowball kept rolling. The dangerous constellation reappeared and the second crisis took place. It is quite possible that the right treatment at the right time could have prevented the deterioration but our job is not to bemoan the past but to reduce the damage to your life and plan for a better future. I believe that now that we've identified your basic vulnerability and the circumstances that endanger you, there is a good chance that we can prevent the same sort of crisis in the future.

The therapy, which lasted intermittently for a few years, helped Eli to achieve more freedom of action and realize his professional potential. Eli became less fearful and inhibited, and his readiness to accept professional and interpersonal challenges grew.

A few years later, the dangerous constellation reappeared. Eli worked nonstop, did not sleep, and coffee and cigarettes were back in large quantities. The therapist was called, but failed to act on time. Eli was hospitalized once again. This time, however, the hospitalization took a different course;

a number of talks between Eli, the therapist, and the psychiatric staff led to a tentative and informal diagnosis of *relapsed stress reaction.* The psychiatrist agreed to the goals of occasioning a minimal disruption in Eli's life, and of conducting the treatment with the full expectation that Eli would return home and go back to work as soon as possible. Eli's condition improved quickly and he was discharged from the hospital after 7 days. In the coming years, there were a number of life crises, but they did not lead to a mental breakdown. On the contrary; Eli withstood the difficulties with courage and resourcefulness. Eli's anger at the way he was treated by the military and the mental-health establishment has not diminished. He feels that his case had been badly botched by a series of indifferent or incompetent professionals. As a result, his life had remained stuck for years. He thinks the best thing that happened to him was to overcome the belief that an incurable illness was lodging within him. He feels that getting rid of this inner phantom gave him the courage and endurance to strive for a better life.

Chapter **4**

Nondemonic Fighting

With Uri Weinblatt

Up until now, we have mostly asked ourselves how people can overcome their demonizing tendencies in situations of psychological threat, from within or from without. But what about situations where there is an objective threat or attack? Is it possible to develop an effective nondemonic defense against actual violence? After all, it is obvious that the attacker harbors, at least temporarily, harmful intentions toward the attacked. Viewing the attacker negatively might then be vital; one must "see red" in order to lash out with all one's might. Fighting without demonizing could then be actually harmful. In our view, however, an effective nondemonic fight is not only feasible, but also potentially more effective and immeasurably less destructive than any fight that is inspired by the demonic outlook.

Conflicts can be managed with varying degrees of destructiveness. Whatever the conflict's scale, from personal fights, through family feuds, to large social clashes, there is a deep difference between forms of conflict management that are guided by attempts to restrain escalation, minimize pain, search for common goals, and preserve the positive elements in the relationship, and forms that are (mis)guided by a willingness to go to extremes, a rejection of any possibility of positive relating, a desire to inflict maximal damage, and a readiness to have third parties or even one's own party pay the price of great suffering and generalized destruction in exchange for the mirage of ultimate victory. The chief question in this chapter is a double one: how to characterize the assumptions of destructive and constructive fighting, and how to lend the constructive approach sufficient appeal to compete with the destructive one even in very acute situations.

When tempers get hot, values like rationality, tolerance, and compassion may be too pale to compete by themselves with the appeal of violent action. In order for these values to have a chance, they must be framed in the context of a highly motivating program of action. People must feel they are being given an option that answers to their strong emotions, recruits them into a decided struggle, and offers them a real prospect of safety. Otherwise, the partisans of rationality, tolerance, and compassion run the risk of falling into helpless resignation, or of swinging over to violence out of despair. We argue that the approach of nonviolent resistance supplies the required action-frame both on the personal and the sociopolitical levels. Within the context of nonviolent resistance, constructive assumptions about the conflict, the adversary, the goals, and the methods of fighting may find the ballast they require to make an impact. The effective counterpart to violence is thus not just the avoidance of violence or the avoidance of fighting, but nonviolent fighting. Nonviolent resistance is decidedly antidemonic both in its practice and in its assumptions.; but it adds one crucial aspect to the so-far described antidemonic attitude: acceptance becomes tempered by decided action.

For 10 years, one of us has conducted a project on the use of nonviolent resistance for helping parents to deal with children's destructive behavior (Omer, 2001, 2004a). Recently, the parental model of nonviolent resistance has been adapted to other settings and kinds of conflict, such as domestic violence against women (Omer, 2004c) and school violence (Omer, Irbauch, & von Schlippe, 2005). The approach has been shown to significantly reduce children's violent behavior at home (Weinblatt, 2004), and in the school. In addition, parental outbursts, parent–child escalation, and offensive behavior by teachers or other members of the school staff have been shown to diminish steeply. These programs aimed not only at the modification of outward behavior but also of the underlying attitudes regarding the conflict. This double attempt at inner and outer change lies also at the heart of the sociopolitical models of nonviolent resistance on which our program was modeled. Leaders like Mahatma Gandhi and Martin Luther King, Jr. developed methods that were aimed at changing both overt acts and inner attitudes. Sharp (1973) systematized the doctrines and strategies of Gandhi and King in ways that make evident the wide scope of the assumptive changes they furthered.

THE ASSUMPTIONS OF DESTRUCTIVE FIGHTING

Destructive kinds of conflict management are based on demonic attributions that explain the conflict as a direct consequence of the opponents' evil qualities. The appeal of this demonic view in acute situations is due to its ability to depict the opponent as a full-fledged enemy, thus offering a clear direction in which to strike. Fear and pain are thus harnessed into militant hatred. Destructive belligerent ideologies, either on a personal or a group level, are thus the warring reflection of the demonic view as a general life philosophy. The assumptions of destructive fighting thus add a new layer to the demonic view; they define the obligatory goals and forms of the fighting, as corollaries of the enemy's assumed nature.

The inner logic of demonization leads to a growing readiness to inflict damage and to suffer it as the necessary price to be paid for defeating the enemy. Sometimes, the levels of demonization and escalation reach such a pitch that both parties come to accept not only the possibility of the enemy's destruction, but also of their own. Demonizing conflicts thus risk turning into apocalyptic wars.

In group forms of demonization, the putative negative essence may be defined in ethnic, biological, social, religious, national, or ideological terms. So long as the members of the opposing group remain what they are (e.g., the Moslems remain Moslem, the Jews remain Jewish, the communists remain communists, etc.), the negative essence will remain active. The destructive potential of this negative essence can be neutralized to the extent that this essence is viewed as removable by a voluntary or forced act (e.g., conversion). However, when no such act is available (e.g., when the putative negative essence is an inborn characteristic), the only way to achieve safety is by instituting strict mechanisms of contact avoidance, such as segregation, banishment, or physical elimination.

In personal conflicts, demonization usually evolves in a different way, because there is often no preconceived idea about the opponent's negative qualities before the conflict develops. Sometimes, the contrary is the case. Thus some of the most intractable divorce battles begin with passionate love stories. Harsh disappointment is then the prelude to hatred. One begins by surmising that the other may hide a negative tendency under her seemingly positive surface. Progressively, this tendency comes to be viewed as the person's defining characteristic: "That is what she really is!" When a state of conflict with the demonized other develops, a whole series of assumptions usually come into play. These assumptions remain the same whether the conflict is waged between individuals, families, groups, or whole societies.

Essential Asymmetry

At the root of most destructive conflicts lies the assumption of basic asymmetry: <u>we</u>[1] are good and <u>they</u> are bad. Even if this assumption is not fully

[1]Throughout the chapter the underlined forms of the pronouns "we" and "they" will denote the opposing parties in the demonic <u>we</u>–<u>they</u> dichotomy.

present from the start, it develops in the course of the hostilities. It is then as if the fighting had revealed the enemy's true nature. Assuming that the enemy is essentially bad justifies one's anger and legitimizes one's blows. In contrast to the enemy's badness, we can feel deep satisfaction at belonging to the good side. This "we feeling" is one of the emotional mainsprings of the demonic approach to conflicts (J. Eidelson, & J. I. Eidelson, 2003; Levine & Campbell, 1976).

The purported asymmetry involves not only a difference in motives, but also in causal processes: whereas their destructive behavior is viewed as being motivated from within, ours is viewed as contextually determined (Pettigrew, 1979). Our war, as opposed to theirs, is thus a noble war, a war of self-defense, or a war to end all wars. The enemy is viewed as solely responsible for the damages, including those that are inflicted on their own side. Sayings like "They brought it upon themselves!" or "They have only themselves to blame!" are used to justify the most extreme policies. Even genocide is staunchly believed to be committed in self-defense (Chirot, 2001). The process of escalation is viewed as one-sided: they escalate, we only react. Paradoxically, the assumption of asymmetry leads to a rigorous symmetry in the conduct of hostilities; both sides feel not only justified, but feel compelled to use the strongest means at their disposal in order to defeat the enemy.

The demonic view postulates that the enemy's negative characteristics are deep and true, but their apparently positive ones are superficial or dissimulatory. This belief biases perception and memory; negative acts, reflecting the enemy's true nature, are perceived and remembered, whereas positive acts are ignored or minimized. Any voices within the enemy camp opposing the violence on their own side are discounted as meaningless. History is equated with one's view of events; the enemy's version is but a willful distortion. Achieving a monopoly over history is crucial; any concession to the enemy's view of events would endanger one's sense of justification. Strong expectations are communicated also to third parties that they should accept the "true" history. All doubts regarding this "truth", either in one's camp or among third parties, reflect ignorance, naiveté, or downright perverseness.

The attempt to gain a monopoly over the description and interpretation of events is no less evident in personal conflicts. Fighting spouses, for instance, usually present totally contradictory versions of the conflict. Attempts to establish a contractual *quid pro quo* (i.e., an agreement in which the spouses commit themselves to parallel positive changes in behavior) often fail, because each side tends to view his or her own positive contributions as far more significant than those of the other. Such agreements often stall on the contention, "I have made a big step; now it's your turn!" If the other protests, saying that he or she is the one who has made the really significant step, the complaining side brings up the demonic argument that the other's positive steps are only external, reflecting no inner change. Also in conflicts between parents and children, a malignant system of bookkeeping often prevails. For instance, some children carry a grudge through life against their parents on grounds of putative discrimination. The parents' attempts to convince the child to give up her grudge, either by bringing contrary evidence or by attempting to satisfy her demands are often discounted or viewed by the child as additional proof that the parents are in deep debt to her. Paradoxically, parental gifts may deepen the grudge and the sense of entitlement. In one of our cases, a 30-year-old woman, who had always claimed that her adoptive parents had deprived her materially and emotionally relatively to their biological son, reacted to their gift of a house by taking the house and accusing them of trying to buy her feelings.

The Obligation to Win

In a demonic fight the outcome must be absolutely univocal and the enemy irrevocably defeated. The zero-sumness of destructive conflicts (Axelrod, 1997; Jervis, 1988) is a corollary of the demonic view, for in a fight with the devil, any concession can be fateful. Zero-sum games forbid outcomes like both sides win, both sides lose, or one side loses little and the other side gains much. Such outcomes would invalidate the black-and-white demonic mindset. The zero-sum assumption implies a paradoxical dependence of the "winner" on the "loser"; because success is only attained with the loser's surrender and full acknowledgment of the winner's superiority, the loser can prevent it by refusing this acknowledgment. Or worse, even a victory that seemed already won can be made to mean nothing if the putative loser withdraws her previous acknowledgment. In this way, the winner must permanently look for reassurances by the loser that her or his superiority is still in place.

The history of many an ethnic and political conflict shows the zero-sum assumption grimly at work. The obligation to win informs the struggle moment by moment, turning the smallest disagreements into life-and-death issues. The interaction becomes dominated by the vocabulary of catastrophe. Even a cursory perusal of the speech of belligerent leaders will show that the word "danger" and its synonyms are the salt of their rhetoric.

Also in intimate fights, winning is experienced as an obligation. Expressions like, "If I give in in this matter, she will think I am weak!" or "If I confess to a mistake, he'll think he's right in everything!" are backed by a truculent determination to make a point. The most virulent fights may then develop out of absolutely trivial matters. Actually, no matter is trivial when viewed through the zero-sum assumption, for even the smallest disadvantage may signify ultimate defeat. In an unsuccessful case of ours, the mother of a 10-year-old boy asked for help with her son's verbal and physical violence toward her. He had frequent tantrums in which he cursed at her, kicked her, and threw things at her. She often hit him and cursed him in return, thus making the event into a symmetrical bout. Her goal in therapy was to stop the boy's violence. She felt that as long as he kept attacking her, she was compelled to hit him back, otherwise he would feel that he had won. In the course of the treatment, she gradually succeeded in resisting the boy's attacks in a nonescalating manner, and for awhile, it seemed that a change was underway. However, after a quiet interval, the boy started making obscene gestures behind her back. The mother viewed this as a very dangerous sign, and the escalation returned in full.

The spirit of symmetry that informs the fight extends beyond the mere "game score." Thus the sides often develop an attitude of rigorous balance that makes them reject all offers of mediation. The contest must remain a strict duel, otherwise, it will be impossible to know who won and who lost. Even good-willed manifestations of this strict symmetrical spirit, such as when the sides demand to solve the problem exclusively by "direct talks," may involve a heavy risk of escalation; this is so because the principled rejection of mediation increases the "duel mentality" and the weight of honor issues, allowing no leeway for face-saving maneuvers. In our parent-training program, we have often observed that the parents' rejection of mediation ("I can definitely say this to him alone!") usually leads to a rapid worsening of the situation.

The Principle of Retaliation

Retaliation is viewed as obligatory and just. It is just, because *they* deserve it, and obligatory, because failing to retaliate means that *we* are letting *them* gain an advantage. The need to retaliate is experienced as a powerful inner drive. A sense of restlessness persists so long as retaliation does not occur. When it does, a fleeting moment of balanced satisfaction may be experienced.

The spirit of retaliation is very close to the spirit of revenge. Revenge is a form of retaliation in which feelings are more important than consequences. Thus, whereas in retaliation, utilitarian considerations still play a part, in revenge they stop doing so. Feelings of revenge are perhaps the only destructive emotions that are experienced with a sense of total moral justification. Revenge is a doubly destructive attitude, for it not only demands destruction of the other, but also accepts the possibility of one's own destruction as its necessary price. The feelings of guilt in revenge are quite peculiar. In contrast to other manifestations of guilt, where guilt usually arouses when one causes pain to others, in revenge, guilt is experienced when one fails to cause pain to others. Guilt is also felt when one proves unwilling to pay the price, for this refusal signifies the neglect of one's highest duty on petty egoistical grounds. Interestingly, revenge is symmetrical only at the beginning; one starts by demanding an eye for an eye, but ends up all the happier if the enemy pays with two eyes or more. The avenger's peace of mind is guaranteed by the belief of not being a free agent; <u>we</u> were drawn into the fray against our will, therefore only <u>they</u> bear the responsibility.

These assumptions are obvious both at the social and the personal level. In divorce, for instance, the parents often draw the children into the fight, in spite of the obvious damage that is inflicted upon the children. Surprisingly, these may often not be "bad" parents at all. In other circumstances, the same parents may be very loving and responsible. This paradox can be explained by the power of the principle of retaliation to effect a radical cleaning of the parents' conscience; both sides feel that they are acting with the highest moral justification, that they are only reacting to aggression, and that they have absolutely no alternative.

The symmetry of "an eye for an eye" entails a honor code with rulings such as (a) ignoring a slight is utterly dishonorable, (b) it is dishonorable to leave a fight in the middle, and (c) offenses can only be paid for by an appropriate atonement. Nisbett and Cohn (1996) linked the prevalence of such honor codes with the frequency of crimes of passion. The honor code is notoriously connected to blood feuds and family vendettas. Less recognized is the role played by implicit honor codes in fueling escalation between adolescents and their parents (Omer, 2004a). In these interactions, each side often assumes that unless the other shows due respect, one loses pride. The offending side must then be forced to change her behavior, or alternatively, be hurt badly enough so as to expiate this behavior. This attitude may be equally common among children as among parents.

The Urge for Total Control

The outcome of the fight should signify one's total control over the opponent, for anything short of that would leave the underlying demonic entity free to restore its powers and pursue its destructive aims. The need for control is derived from fear, and is experienced as stemming purely from self-defense. Those who strive for total control almost invariably feel that they are in the grip of an overwhelming force (Lake & Rotchild, 1998).

In different circumstances, four outcomes may represent the desired degree of control: (a) *conversion*—by this is meant the full and unconditional acceptance of "the truth" by the adversary. Care should be taken to reject mere external adaptations. Contrition, confession, and acknowledgment of guilt are necessary stages in the process of conversion that show that the proffered acceptance is not only lip service. When the fight is under way, it is not expected that conversion will occur spontaneously; however, it can result from the opponents' acknowledgment of their absolute powerlessness and inferiority; (b) *subjugation*—it is assumed that force is the only language the enemy understands. Most demonic contenders share the strange hope that force will, in fact, bring "understanding." If, however, the enemy fails to understand, one of the following outcomes may be necessary: (c) *expulsion*—the negative destructive elements must be purged. In this process of purification, the wheat is separated from the chaff and the putative demonic essences are cast off (e.g. in exorcism or banishment); (d) *elimination*—the enemy should be destroyed.

In personal relations, these forms of control may create a continuum of intimate destructiveness. Consider the escalatory potential of conversion attempts. Rebellious children or wives, for instance, should be made to accept inwardly the parents' or husband's truth. However, most attempts to hammer the truth into the mind of a "stubborn" spouse or child are usually not only ineffective but also escalatory. In these situations, resolute persuasion gives way to threats, threats to punishments, and punishments to retaliation (Omer, 2004a). Adolescents are particularly apt to interpret parental attempts at persuasion as the parent's aiming for total control. Thus understood, the parents' attempts are often experienced as even more invasive than the harshest punishments. In marital violence, attempts to convince by verbal reprimands often precede the appeal to naked force. The battering man commonly views his violence as a last resource after all other attempts to bring the woman to the right mind have failed. In these situations, making the woman "understand" is experienced not as an option, but as a must. It is precisely this compulsion to convince that turns the persuasive attempt into a nondialogue, for if the other proves adamant in his or her thinking, the use of force is seen as inevitable. The two outcomes (conversion and subjugation) thus merge into one another. When conversion and subjugation fail, the threat of expulsion may come into play. At the extreme of this continuum, the options of banishment for life or homicide may become relevant.

Suspicion and Secretiveness

The ruling attitude is one of pervasive suspicion. Suspicion is not merely a spontaneous reaction, but a duty; not to suspect means dropping one's guard, thus allowing the enemy to take one by surprise. Disbelieving the adversary's seemingly positive acts or declarations is a sign of realistic responsibility; failing to do so is proof of wishful thinking and moral laxness (J. Eidelson, & J. I. Eidelson, 2003; Kramer, & Messick, 1998). To detect the enemy's ever-present scheming, one must learn to interpret signs of scheming.

Thus, in demonic group conflicts, specialists or institutions that are held able to uncover the enemy's plots usually stand at the top of the social hierarchy. The work of these specialists is directed not only at the external enemy but also at the enemy within. The "secret police" is thus a corollary of the demonic view.

The emotional appeal of suspiciousness might seem puzzling. After all, trust seems to be a more comfortable attitude. And yet, in situations of conflict, suspicion is not only experienced as reasonable, but is also a source of emotional gratification. By suspicion, individuals or groups overcome the sense that they are fools or passive victims; they develop a feeling of superiority, as they "uncover" the antagonists' secret schemes, and they increase their own sense of justification and entitlement. Paraphrasing the title of a famous story, we might say that, "A good enemy is hard to find."[2] With the appropriate work of suspicion, however, marvelous enemies can be found.

Suspicion and secretiveness go hand in hand, for dealing openly in a fight with the devil is tantamount to playing into his hands. It is imperative to hide one's goals and strategies, both from the enemy and from potential critics. No one causes greater indignation in the fighter with a demonic mindset than the inner critic who publicizes the doings within her own party. Washing one's laundry in public is viewed as the grossest betrayal, both in group and in family conflicts. Needless to say, secrecy inspires a symmetrical attitude in the opponent.

The Immediacy Principle

Every moment is crucial and every encounter fateful, for the smallest tilt of the balance might lead to the establishment of a fixed hierarchy. At every instant, both sides seem to think: "If I come out stronger now, I am at the top!" Any delay or hesitation risks giving the enemy a chance to strike first. The smashing blow epitomizes the ideal solution, for attempting to win the fight in a more gradual manner or with less force would actually involve more suffering and more risk. If, as it usually turns out, the expected smashing blow proves disappointing, a more decisive blow must be implemented. The belief that each and every encounter determines the winner and the loser leads to a selective blindness to gradual processes. Events that require ripening or growth are ignored, for they do not define the winner on an immediate basis. The history of the interaction becomes the history of its battles, each of which is viewed as ultimative at the time of its occurrence. The *immediacy principle* thus leads to an extremely narrow time-perspective: All efforts that are not invested on winning the battle here and now are viewed as wasteful. Destructive conflicts are thus a series of "now or never" at-

---

[2]Flannery O'Connor's *A Good Man is Hard to Find.*

tempts. Because smashing blows are seldom really smashing, the series may prove interminable.

The emotional appeal of the immediacy principle is linked to the psychophysiology of arousal; arousal makes one ready to strike. A view of the conflict that calls for lashing out with full might at the pitch of one's anger thus receives a clear boost from the hormones. Delaying the strike is like swimming against the stream.

The principle of immediacy supplies the drumbeat of war rhetoric. It is also paramount in personal conflicts, where any delay is believed to convey weakness. The principle of immediacy often informs the contestants' intuitive learning theory. In this view, if punishment is not administered on the spot, it loses its instructive potential. The interaction thus becomes ruled by a sense of total urgency. Nothing ever has a chance to develop.

THE APPEAL OF THE DEMONIC APPROACH TO FIGHTING

In his classic biography of Erasmus, Stefan Zweig drew a bleak picture of the ineptitude of humanist values to stand against fanaticism in times of social upheaval (Zweig 1935/1982). Zweig described how at such times, the winds blow so strongly that the world becomes like a cloth that is torn in two by the warring parties. The would-be bystander loses his footing and, for good or ill, must take a clear stand for one of the sides. Humane values must then bow to the urgency of fanatic ideals, far-sighted goals pale before immediate ones, and the capacity for ambiguity gives way to the need for absolute certainty. At these junctures, only group-rootedness and the hatred of the common enemy seem to provide meaning and enable action.

Besides their ability to galvanize arousal, the destructive assumptions help to create turbulence, transforming otherwise limited conflicts into the total conflagrations for which they then pose as the unique solution. The destructive assumptions thus work as self-fulfilling prophecies that draw the wavering more and more into the widening circle of hatred.

Consider, for instance, the assumption of essential asymmetry: assuming that a hidden negative essence rules the opponent's behavior entails a special yardstick for judging his acts. The negative interpretation is thus self-reinforcing, invariably strengthening the belief that the enemy is built of different stuff altogether. These processes create a mood in which safety is only experienced when one feels one is not being duped. Thus, viewing the enemy's acts in a wholly negative light paradoxically increases one's sense of security.

The assumption of zero-sumness is equally self-reinforcing. On this view, any goal they may happen to pursue must be highly desirable to us. The fact that they want something is reason enough to fight tenaciously for it. One of the bleakest examples of this logic is the Battle of Verdun in World War I (Taylor, 1966). The original German plan regarding Verdun was to stage a series of sham attacks, so that the French would believe the Germans viewed Verdun as crucial for their war strategy. The French would then react by creating a large concentration of forces in that single area. This would allow the Germans to bleed the French through artillery attacks, without offering a comparably vulnerable concentration of manpower. Documents from the German general command showed that, at this stage, the Germans did not view the conquest of Verdun as at all central for their war effort, but only as the ideal place to cause the French as many losses as possible. However, the decision of the French to defend Verdun by all possible means persuaded the Germans that Verdun was really vital. This led to a change in the German plans; they now came to the conclusion that the conquest of Verdun was imperative! Their logic seemed to be, "If the French want it so much, we should want it too!" As the battle progressed, anyone in the German staff who failed to understand that Verdun was worth the utmost sacrifice would be in danger of being demoted.

A similar mental exercise could be conducted with each of the destructive assumptions. In the kind of reality they create, moral scruples are signs of cowardice. The advocates of compromise, dialogue, and conciliation become the targets of hostility and ridicule. Even the enemy deserves more respect than they do. They are the lukewarm, cowardly, spineless crowd, that in Dante's *Divine Comedy* are spurned equally by Heaven and by Hell.

In this atmosphere, occasional glimmerings of humaneness and rationality may end by paradoxically increasing the hold of the destructive assumptions. If, for a while, a chance is given to the apostles of dialogue to try their hand at achieving a solution, a few violent outbursts may suffice, as showing the enemy's "true face." A return to unrestrained violence is then felt as doubly justified. This backlash of the demonic view after the failure of a peaceful attempt characterizes both sociopolitical and personal conflicts. In the Israeli–Palestinian conflict, for instance, once in awhile the partisans of compromise are given a chance. However, when violence succeeds in interrupting the dialogue, the sides usually go back to a very lengthy bout of mutual destructiveness. Endless sacrifices may then be needed until a readiness for dialogue gingerly reappears. A similar process characterizes protracted personal conflicts. Thus, in marital conflicts a chance may be given once in awhile to positive dialogue. However, a few disappointments may suffice for the fight to erupt again in all its harshness. Eventually, even the believers in gentle methods may come to believe that only force can do the job.

In times of turmoil, the destructive assumptions thus seem to have a clear edge over the voices of reason. Moreover, because the demonic view aptly stirs up the chaos it needs in order to thrive, the dice seem to be heavily loaded in its favor. To redress this imbalance, a constructive approach to conflict management should offer a more full-blooded alternative than the mere advocacy of the ideals of humaneness, tolerance, and rationality. Actually, no less than a highly motivating, but strictly nonviolent fighting program could compete with the highly motivating demonic assumptions.

THE ASSUMPTIONS OF CONSTRUCTIVE FIGHTING

Far from being an esoteric approach that could flourish only in an exceptionally nonbelligerent culture, nonviolent resistance has been utilized throughout history by the most varied social and ethnic groups (Sharp, 1973). The basic idea of nonviolent resistance is a very common one: "I'll defend myself with all possible means but without striking back!" What turns this everyday idea into a most powerful tool is the development of a set of principles and strategies that turn it into a clearly defined and well-organized approach to fighting.

The Obligation to Resist

The nonviolent counterpart of the obligation to win is the obligation to resist. Although violence should be rigorously abjured, no bones should be made about the fact that nonviolent resistance involves power and is decidedly a form of fighting. Gandhi stressed that those who avoid all recourse to power as a matter of principle actually perpetuate violence and oppression. In his view, demands or entreaties that are not backed by power and by a full readiness to resist have no influence (Sharp, 1960). The attempt to behave toward a violent opponent exclusively by empathic understanding, conciliation, and verbal persuasion actually risks making things worse, for these attitudes are often viewed by the violent side as signifying surrender. Surrender, in turn, increases the aggressor's readiness to use threats and force. This kind of escalation has been termed *complementary*, whereas the kind of escalation in which hostility engenders hostility has been termed *symmetrical* (Bateson, 1972; Orford, 1986). Nonviolent resistance counters both complementary and symmetrical escalation.

Without the option of nonviolent resistance, the victims of aggression will oscillate between surrender and violence. Thus, in oppressive societies, periods of total subjugation are usually punctured by violent uprisings. Since the oppressive yoke tends to grow heavier in the wake of an uprising, the ground is laid to yet another uprising. This oscillation is no less evident in the personal sphere. Thus, the parents of aggressive children often alternate between a policy of appeasement (buying quiet) and recourse to harsh and often physical punishments (Omer, 2004a, Weinblatt, 2005). Nonviolent resistance acts as a brake on this harmful oscillation; one resists violence continuously, thus avoiding the despair that often unleashes the conflict's full destructiveness.

The obligation to resist has received little attention in the field of domestic violence. Answers to domestic violence are either attempts at therapy (of the aggressor, the victim, or both), or attempts to disconnect the victim from the aggressor. When both fail, therapists and other social agents may become helpless. The lack of professional attention to steps of resistance has probably a double cause: an antiauthoritarian aversion to meddling with power and a dearth of practical tools. Both can be remedied by an appropriate adaptation of nonviolent resistance in the family sphere. The warm response to our program of nonviolent resistance to child-violence[3] seems to show that the program successfully addressed the double root of professional helplessness; it offered convincing nonviolent tools and addressed the issue of power without an authoritarian stance (Omer, 2004a).

Basic Similarity and Many-Voicedness

Instead of assuming that they are bad and we are good, nonviolent resistance postulates that on both sides positive and negative voices coexist. Some of these voices, even if temporarily weak or dormant, can be assumed to oppose the use of violence. Mahatma Gandhi and Martin Luther King, Jr. were past masters at strengthening the antiviolence voices in both camps. To this end, they emphasized that the enemy is not the opposing group: one must fight against oppression and violence, not against the British or the Whites. Blaming the British or the Whites would only increase the power and cohesion of the violent voices in their camp. The same considerations are relevant for dealing with the aggressive spouse, child, or parent; viewing the other's behavior as influenced by multiple inner voices allows one to strengthen the nonviolent ones, instead of weakening them by discounting them as meaningless.

This vision of the opponent as many-voiced is both optimistic and realistic. It is optimistic in that positive voices, even if hard to discern, are always assumed to be present. It is realistic in the acknowledgment that the nonviolent resistor's endeavor cannot bring about the total disappearance of the negative voices. Actually there is no need to do so. It may suffice to tip the balance in favor of the positive ones.

In the study of suicide, the expression, "the parliament of the mind," was coined to indicate that within the potential suicide, many voices coexist,

---

[3] This applies to Israel, Germany, Switzerland, and Brazil, where the program was presented to professionals, occasioning a high demand for courses, supervision, and written materials.

some favoring life. The helper's chief aim should not be the rather unrealistic one of making the potential suicide embrace life unconditionally, but that of gaining a majority for the life voices (Shneidman, 1985). Sometimes, even a tiny change in the right direction may suffice. Similarly, in the field of conflict management, regarding the adversary's destructive behavior as a result of a debate within his inner "parliament of the mind" leads to the formulation of a more realistic goal than that of eliminating the ultimate roots of violence. The new goal is to create a majority for the antiviolence voices.

In adopting this assumption, one undertakes not to discount the adversary's positive acts as nonsignificant, manipulative, or dissembling. On the contrary, each positive act is a manifestation of a positive voice that merits our respect and support. One's reaction to these positive manifestations may well determine whether they will be strengthened or weakened.

Also in one's own camp a multiplicity of voices is assumed to be present, requiring a continuous effort against the voices of violence. Nonviolent resistance demands that violence be abjured not as a tactical move, but as a matter of principle. However, it is assumed that so long as the conflict persists, the violent voices may occasionally gain the upper hand. Occasional bouts of violence may thus puncture one's nonviolent stance, requiring a renewed commitment to nonviolence. To maintain this commitment, it is necessary to develop endurance and learn to withstand provocations. Interestingly, this ethos of endurance, far from discouraging the resistors, enhances their motivation (Sharp, 1973). Also in personal situations, the commitment to endurance proves self-enhancing; parents feel much strengthened when they successfully withstand the child's provocations (Omer, 2004a; Weinblatt, 2005). There is thus a pride and a pleasure in endurance that allow it to compete with the releasing effects of violent anger.

The assumption of multivoicedness has an additional appeal; it sustains the belief that the positive elements in the relationship can be salvaged. In many conflicts, positive memories and present shimmerings stay on in spite of the ruling hostility. The demonic view is threatened by these inklings and endeavors to eliminate them. The suppression of the positive, however, can be very painful. In this respect, the assumption of multivoicedness is a boon; it is highly encouraging that the positive is not lost, but can be nurtured and fostered, even while one is most immersed in the work of resisting.

Leaders like Gandhi and King did not settle for the absence of violence alone. They demanded that the acts of resistance be accompanied, as far as humanly possible, by respect and positive relating. The assumption that the antagonist merits respect and that even at the pitch of resistance, one must find place for positive steps is a logical consequence of the assumption of multivoicedness. However, the positive offers of the nonviolent resistor are very different from what is usually meant by "appeasement." Whereas appeasement consists in conciliation to the adversary by giving in to his threats, the positive steps of Gandhi and King are freely chosen offers of positive regard within a context of continuing resistance.

These ideas are perhaps even more relevant for intimate conflicts, where positive feelings often live on in spite of the fighting. Thus, in our program for the parents of violent children, the parents are coached to make reconciliation gestures even on the very days in which they are most engaged in the work of resistance. Surprisingly, parents often report that the reconciliation gestures increased their ability to resist. By these steps, they show to themselves and to the child that they are respectful and loving resistors! The mix of resistance with reconciliation has also had a positive effect on escalation (de Waal, 1993; Weinblatt, 2004, 2005). This could be interpreted as meaning that reconciliation steps succeed in diminishing the violent voices in the "inner parliament" of both sides. Reconciliation represents a move away from the zero-sumness that underlies destructive fighting. In a zero-sum game, if the adversary receives an unearned prize, one's side is disadvantaged. For this reason, parents are sometimes stymied by the proposal to engage in reconciliation steps ("But she doesn't deserve it!"). In a non-zero-sum game, however, both sides may gain from an "undeserved" reconciliation gesture. Thus, as the parents experiment with reconciliation, they gradually wean themselves from zero-sumness.

Asymmetry of Means

Instead of the compelling symmetry of retaliation, the nondemonic fighter opts for a systematic asymmetry of means; violence is met with nonviolent and nonescalating resistance. In nonviolent resistance, a *violent act* is defined tangibly as one that involves inflicting physical or emotional harm to the opponent. This definition of violence does not include actions whose aim is to disable the destructive activities of the violent side but do not inflict direct physical or mental harm. These actions are precisely the ones that characterize the stance of the activists as *resistance.*

When faced with nonviolent resistance, violence tends to become ineffective and self-limiting. Violence is robbed of its strength for various reasons: (a) it loses legitimacy; (b) it may undergo inhibition by the opponents' nonviolent stance; (c) its confidence is shaken by the message of endurance conveyed by nonviolent resistance; and (d) the asymmetry of means brings in support for the nonviolent side. By these processes, nonviolent resistance creates an environment in which violence finds it hard to survive. However, the nonviolent side must not assume that renouncing violence will make the antagonist give up violence quickly. Such a belief would turn nonviolent resistance into a mere tactical maneuver, to be discarded if the opponent continued to behave violently. The asymmetry of means is a principled choice; in opting for it, one must evolve a readiness to go on resisting without lashing back, even in the face of persisting violence.

The nonviolent fighter views escalation as a mutual process and the avoidance of retaliation as a crucial step in breaking its grip. According to the demonic view, escalation is the inevitable result of the enemy's master plan. Viewing escalation as a mutual process works as an antidote against this belief. The very question, "Who is to blame?" or "Who started it?" tends to strengthen the demonic mind-set. The question is usually pointless, as there are always two incompatible narratives with different starting points and sets of facts. Even when there is an obvious aggressor, the symmetric spirit that demands a strict cancellation of all past hurts may trigger an escalating spiral that far outweighs the original damage. The novel, *Michael Kolhaas*, by Heinrich von Kleist (1978) tells of a justice-loving squire who was the victim of an arbitrary act of exploitation; two of his horses were taken from him by cheating and made to work the fields of the local strong man, who then derisively offered to give them back to him in a decrepit state. Kolhaas, whose initial attempts to get compensation by legal means failed, decided to get his due by force. He gathered a band of desperados and led a revolt, in the course of which farms and towns were razed to the ground, his wife was murdered, he was sent to the scaffold, and his children were sent to orphanages. Throughout the story, each time Kolhaas was asked about his demands, he answered, "I want my horses back exactly as they were!"

The Illusion of Control

The belief that one can control the other's behavior or determine her feelings is illusory. We only have some direct influence over our own acts, but our influence over the other person's is, at best, very partial and indirect. The assumption that control over the other is illusory may have a liberating effect; one becomes freed from the compulsion to control by the awareness that control is impossible. The assumptions of nonviolent resistance thus merge with the tragic view. Nonviolent fighting is not contaminated by the hubris of control.

Focusing one's efforts on one's own, rather than at the opponent's behavior, creates the deepest difference between nonviolent and violent fighting. A typical threat issued in the spirit of violence has the form of a strict logical implication: "If you don't do what I say, I will hurt you!" The emphasis is on a strong linkage between the acts. The opponent is given two options: to comply or to be punished. In order to maintain his standing, the opponent must refuse to comply, preferably issuing an escalating counter threat. In contrast, a typical message in nonviolent resistance is, "I will resist, because I must!" The emphasis is placed on the duty of resisting and not on control over the other person. If the opponent answers by a threat, the resistor reiterates his obligation to resist.

Gandhi expressed this spirit of determination without control in a letter to Lord Irwin, the British Viceroy, in which he communicated his decision to resist the British salt monopoly. After declaring that India had the duty to do all in her power to free herself from the "embrace of death" of the British Empire, Gandhi declared that he and his followers had no alternative but to initiate a wide-ranging campaign of nonviolent resistance against the monopoly. He ended the letter paradoxically: "This letter is not in anyway intended as a threat but as a simple and sacred duty peremptory on a civil resister" (Sharp, 1960, pp. 200–204). The paradox consists in the simultaneous announcement of a fighting campaign and the declaration that this was no threat. The paradox may however be resolved, if we compare Gandhi's declaration with an ordinary threat: (a) threats do not usually include an explicit declaration of nonviolence; (b) Gandhi does not say, "You will do this, or else ...," but "We have no choice, but ... "; and (c) there is no hint of willfulness in Gandhi's words ("This is what I want!"), but an expression of moral duty. Gandhi's declaration could be paraphrased as follows: "You are stronger than I am, but my supreme duty is to resist you in a nonviolent way!" Gandhi's message can therefore be characterized as "a threat in a nonthreatening spirit." Such a message is free of the need to show to the other "who is the boss."

The same dynamics are manifested in personal conflicts. The need for control and the belief in control's possibility leads one to view the relationship in terms of, "Who's the boss?" The more pronounced this tendency, the greater the danger of escalation. Thus parents who tended to view the relationship in terms of "Who's the boss?" were found to be particularly viable to violent outbursts (Bugental, Blue, & Cruzcosa, 1989, Bugental, et al., 1993, Bugental, Lyon, Krantz, & Cortez, 1997). This holds true for the control-minded child as well; the more she thinks in terms of "Who's the boss?" the more will she be prone to violent outbursts. If one of the sides in the relationship (in our project, the parent) succeeds in curbing her or his own control-mindedness, the danger of escalation decreases. In our parent-training program, parents learn to convey messages like, "I cannot control you! But I will resist your violence by all nonviolent means at my disposal," or "I cannot defeat you! But I will do my best to protect myself" (Omer, 2001, 2004a). The emotional effect of such messages can be considerable. Optimally, both sides may be gradually freed from the compulsion to make a point.

This change in focus from the other to the self has an additional bonus. The demonic state of mind consists of a *negative hypnosis*, in which one becomes fascinated and enthralled by the other's bad characteristics; one cannot stop cataloguing the opponent's negative acts. As long as this litany persists, one does not feel free to act, but is compelled to focus on the other person, react to her, and complain of her doings. One's own voice loses power as the mind becomes filled with the imagined negative voice of the other. In giving up the illusion of control, it is possible to break free from this negative hypnosis; we now focus on our own acts. In our work with parents, we often witness a change in the parents' way of talking; whereas in the initial sessions they almost always open the session by a long list of complaints about the child's unacceptable doings, as treatment progresses they report first of all on their own steps of resistance and self-protection.

Publicity

Transparency and publicity inhibit violence (on both sides) and allow for the mobilization of support for the nonviolent camp. For this reason, movements of nonviolent resistance operate in ways that are diametrically opposed to those of underground organizations, opting for publicity and rejecting secrecy. Opting for publicity may be far from simple, but so long as one chooses to keep things secret, one may be contributing to the perpetuation of violence. This is clearest in the family; all forms of domestic violence are abetted by secrecy. Gandhi added another reason for opting unconditionally for publicity: Secretiveness stems from fear, and is bound to perpetuate fear. Thus, instead of helping overcome paralysis, the habits of mind engendered by secrecy actually deepen it. Yet another reason for favoring publicity is that it creates a public commitment to abide by nonviolence. Publicity is thus a key element not only in the fight against the adversary's destructive acts, but also against one's own destructive acts.

Publicity is crucial for the mobilization of a support net. The lonely resistor has virtually no power, and is easily the prey of fear and demoralization. The situation changes when the individual breaks out of isolation. Many have marveled at the courage of nonviolent activists on the face of extremely repressive measures. Gandhi stressed that this courage is not born out of the lonely individual's soul, but out of the experience of togetherness. The very dialogue that makes victims aware that the oppression is arbitrary is a result of togetherness. Breaking out of isolation is no less crucial in family violence. Victims of family violence are helpless so long as they stay alone and the violence remains hidden. Going open about the violence is an act of revolutionary impact; at one stroke, the forlornness of the victim is shaken off. Protection of the victim and public pressure against violence become possible.

Publicity is the key to a form of nonviolent resistance that is relevant even under the most extreme kinds of oppression—the giving of testimony. The high value of testimony for the victims of violence has been shown in cases of extreme oppression, such as among victims of the military dictatorship in Chile, of racial apartheid in South Africa, or within the starving confines of the Warsaw Ghetto. Giving testimony allows the victims to be acknowledged as victims and to feel that their suffering has potential meaning to others. Testimony is quite different from therapeutic disclosure; the latter is usually a private event, whereas testimony is a public one. This point is seldom understood by professionals. Thus, the attention of therapists is usually focused on the inner work of "processing," in disregard of the high-supportive and therapeutic value of a potentially large sympathetic audience.[4] In our program, we try to persuade victimized siblings, women, and parents, to document their sufferings (in writing or on tape), and present these sufferings before an audience of supporters (members of the extended family, friends, other victims, or therapeutic staff). Some of the victims who are reluctant to come out into the open sometimes agree to have their testimony circulated anonymously. By these means, they begin to view themselves as resistors. The option of testimony greatly increases the emotional appeal of nonviolent resistance (Omer, 2004b; Omer, Shor-Sapir, & Weinblatt, in press). Survivors of the Warsaw Ghetto have described how the ghetto's inmates who came in contact with Emanuel Ringelblum (the historian who documented the ghetto's oppression) were often willing to undergo severe hardships in order to amass documents that would bear witness to the world about what they went through. The effect of this work of testimony on the victims' morale was immense (e.g., Reich-Ranicki, 2003).

The togetherness of nonviolent resistance is very different from the togetherness that is fostered by the demonic approach to conflict. The latter is a closed togetherness, built out of a "we–they" contrasting polarity. The nonviolent variety is an open togetherness that invites third parties and also members from the opposing group to join in. In a project on nonviolent resistance in schools, an open front against violence was built through a teacher–parent alliance based on the principle that every act of violence and its disciplinary treatment would be publicized (without the children's names) in a biweekly letter to the parents, teachers, and children. Talks were then conducted in each class, in which the children were invited to join the open front against bullying, vandalism, and other forms of violence (Omer, 2004; Omer, Irbauch, & von Schlippe, 2005). These talks aimed at abrogating the tacit rule of silence, which prevented most children from reporting on the violence they witnessed. All the children, including those that had previously behaved as bullies, could now view themselves as members of the new we that actively re-

[4] An important exception is the work of Michael White (1997, 2000).

sisted violence. Gradually, many of the kids that had been previously identified as bullies were found to have changed their alliance.

The Principle of Ripeness

In contrast to the immediacy principle, it is assumed that the contest is not a power test defining an incontrovertible hierarchy, but part of an ongoing process that continuously redefines the quality of the relationship. Attempts to defeat and subjugate, far from leading to a stable outcome, lead to a deterioration of the relationship. Therefore, the goal of the nonviolent resistor is not to achieve an immediate resolution, but to persevere until the positive processes ripen. The nonviolent resistor fights tenaciously but without the expectation that the opponent will desist from violence in the short run. The ethos of endurance of nonviolent resistance represents the total opposite of the belief in a decisive blow.

The principle of ripeness involves a reeducation of attention. One learns to attend also to minute positive events, allowing these the opportunity to mature. This contrasts deeply with the negative hypnosis of the destructive fighter, in which fascination with the negative leads to a systematic disregard of the positive.

The principle of ripeness involves also a modification of the positive expectations. The tempered nonviolent fighter knows full well that attempting to force a positive solution may prove abortive, often leading the sides to swing over to destructive solutions. Nonviolent resistors school themselves in long-winded endurance, attend to slowly maturing changes, sedulously cultivate potential allies, are suspicious of the mirage of ultimate victory, are skeptical about push-button control, and are modest in their immediate goals. The high hopes that inspire the destructive fighter would probably prove more attractive to many. But the staying power of the nonviolent resistor outlives disappointments better.

THE POWER OF THE NONVIOLENT APPROACH TO FIGHTING

The high appeal of nonviolent resistance is linked to its ability to harness the victims' despair and indignation into a resolute and persistent nondemonic fighting endeavor. This channeling of pain into resistance contrasts with the relative unpractical character of many otherwise positive ideologies in situations of acute conflict. The power-averse apostles of humane ideals often fail to mobilize victims to a real fight against violence, thereby being relegated to the status of prophets in the desert. Not so the proponents of nonviolent resistance, who actually build on the arousal and indignation that are ignited by violence and oppression. This motivating power has been often demonstrated in the sociopolitical arena, where movements of nonviolent resistance have sometimes reached mass proportions, and where social groups that had previously been viewed either as naturally subservient or incurably bellicose refuted all expectations and displayed an amazing ability to resist and to abstain from violence (Sharp, 1973). Experience with the parents of violent children shows a similar picture; previously helpless and seemingly unmotivated parents react positively when the determined stance and strategy of nonviolent resistance is presented to them. This motivational surge grows steadier and stronger with the parents' first experiences in resistance. This is attested by the fact that parental drop-out rates from the program of nonviolent resistance are probably the lowest in the whole parent-training literature (Weinblatt, 2005). The mobilization of the parents often spreads to others. Friends and members of the extended family are quick to join in, further strengthening the parents' commitment. In the extremely delicate area of violence against siblings, mobilization of the parents and of other supporters is often followed by a successful recruitment of the victimized siblings into the resistance program. The enthusiastic response of these previously completely helpless children is a pledge for the wide relevance of the approach (Omer, Shor-Sapir, & Weinblatt, in press).

Nonviolent resistance is not a spontaneous reaction to oppression and violence. There is something more "natural" about hitting back or even giving in. These two options are, as it were, programmed by evolution, whereas nonviolent resistance is a cultural product. Nonviolent resistance has to be perceived as an option—planned, organized, and set in motion. Because of these complex demands, it requires a trained leadership. The role of the leaders is to acquaint the potential followers with the nonviolent ideas, help define the goals of resistance, organize its strategies, reach out for supporters, train the participants, and guarantee their self-restraint. This is true for the sociopolitical as well as the family arena. The complexity of these tasks turns nonviolent leadership into a quasi professional role. However, the enthusiasm that is often aroused by its messages enables a wide recruitment of potential new leaders.

The strong response aroused by nonviolent resistance is partly due to its surprise value. In the cognitive map of most people, fighting and violence belong together, so that the perceived options are usually: fighting (violently) versus surrendering, fighting versus conciliating, or fighting versus talking. Unfortunately, the nonviolent alternatives in these pairs may be quite unhelpful. The option of nonviolent resistance may then have a high impact; reality becomes newly mapped, allowing for significant action where none was perceived before. In this new mapping, the once-incompatible pair, fighting and nonviolence become joined together.

Responses like, "Why didn't we think of this before?" or "Why do you call this *fighting* if it is nonviolent?" testify to the surprise evoked by the new representation. As the compatibility between fighting and nonviolence dawns, a motivational surge often becomes manifest.

The next stage is the training of the resistors. Gandhi remarked that the tempering of the activists can be a quick process, as the very first experiences in resisting often transform even deeply resigned victims into decided fighters. This transformation is often witnessed in the family arena as well. Thus, after conducting a first "sit-in" in the violent child's room, parents often express surprise that they were able to manage it. One mother remarked that her muscles had remained tense for the whole hour of the sit-in. She then added, "But now I know that I have muscles!" Even the experience of physical pain may undergo a metamorphosis. After a few weeks in a program of resistance against her older brother's violence, a 12-year-old girl said, "Sometimes he still hits me! But now it doesn't hurt so much!"

The appeal of nonviolent resistance is also fed by the changes that begin appearing on the violent side. A disorganization of the process of violence often becomes evident, showing that violence cannot cope well with an opponent who neither hits back nor gives in. This disorganization strengthens the resistors. The first time an oppressive policy is called back is a significant historical marker for any movement of nonviolent resistance. This is further abetted by the emergence of protesting voices in the violent camp that oppose violence and support the resistors. Occasionally, even the onetime upholders of violence begin to show a change of heart. We term this process *identification with the nonaggressor.*

Gradually, the feelings of inferiority that made oppression possible give way to a sense of personal and moral superiority. This is strengthened by publicity and by support from third parties.

Nonviolence resistance is thus a self-reinforcing process. Those who experience this form of fighting will find it hard to return to the ways of violence. The readiness of individuals and groups to embrace nonviolent resistance is a function of their acquaintance with the idea and of the availability of a clear program of action. Once these conditions are fulfilled, nonviolent resistance competes well with the alternatives of violent fighting and passive resignation. Furthermore, each new application of nonviolent resistance in the sociopolitical or the family arenas increases people's awareness about its possibility. The option of violence, in contrast, is obvious to everyone, and its popularity does not necessarily grow by new applications. Hopefully, this expanding consciousness will gradually tilt the balance in favor of nonviolent resistance.

NONDEMONIC FIGHTING IN ACTION: NONVIOLENT RESISTANCE BY THE PARENTS OF VIOLENT CHILDREN AND YOUTH

Our program of nonviolent resistance for the parents of violent and self-destructive children and youth includes detailed practical instructions on how to prevent escalation, mobilize support, implement resistance measures, protect the victims (and the aggressive child), and increase parental presence in areas where the problem child engages in high-risk activities (Omer, 2004a).

It might seem strange that we chose the relations between parents and children as our chief illustration of nondemonic fighting. After all, parents are not supposed to fight with their children. The very need to do so may give ground to the suspicion that they have somehow failed as parents. However, even the most devoted of parents may discover to their astonishment that some children and especially adolescents behave violently or self-destructively in spite of the love and care they have received. The parents may then wonder whether the child's behavior is due to underlying psychopathological or basic violent tendencies. Both explanations assume that a negative essence or implant lodges within the child. If the child is viewed as harboring violent tendencies, the parents may feel justified in using harsh educational methods, so as to make her understand or show her who's the boss. This often leads to symmetric escalation. On the other hand, if the child is viewed as psychologically ill, the parents may veer toward appeasement and giving in, which often leads to complementary escalation (i.e., the more yielding the parents, the harsher the child's behavior). The demonic explanation of the child's negative behaviors in terms of inner qualities or implants spills over to the parents. Thus, the parents are often blamed by outsiders or by each other for having caused the destructiveness. Many parents also blame themselves. The parents' failings are then explained by demonic hypotheses, for instance, that the parents carry traumatic scars from their own childhood, or that they are mentally or morally unfit. The assumptions of nonviolent resistance serve as an antidote to these attributions; the child is viewed as not necessarily deficient either in a moral or a psychological way, and the parents as not necessarily neglectful or abusive. It is assumed instead that both sides got caught in a tragic spiral of negative reactions in spite of intentions and feelings that might have been originally positive and adaptive.

Many of the parents who came to the parent-training program often tried to solve the child's problems by ineffective attempts at conciliation, or by downright giving in. These attempts were punctured by mutual verbal violence, which might also deteriorate into erratic punishments or physical outbursts. The parents' sense of helplessness grew with each new failed attempt. They complained that the child reacted neither to the "hard way" (scolding, screaming, punishing), nor to the "soft way" (acceptance, appeasement, and therapy for the child). They usually viewed the situation as a zero-sum gain, in which they always "lost" and the child "won". The program's goal was to train them in nonviolent resistance, as an antidote both to giving in and to hitting back. A major emphasis was the attempt to help them perceive, recognize, and encourage positive voices and events.

The parents were coached on the implementation of a series of resistance steps, such as (a) making an open declaration of resistance and nonviolence; (b) performing sit-ins; (c) protecting themselves, the children, and the house; (d) refusing to comply with threats; (e) breaking out of secrecy; and (f) mobilizing a support net. They were also trained on how to avoid behaviors with a high risk of escalation, such as, entreaties, admonishments, arguments, accusations, threats, screams, spankings, and humiliating remarks or punishments. They learned to withstand the child's provocations and not to react immediately to aggressive acts. Delaying their response allowed them to avoid the trap of high emotional arousal. An attitude of patient persistence was cultivated and contraposed to expectations of immediate change. The parents were also encouraged to perform reconciliation steps toward the child, in parallel with the ongoing resistance and independent of the child's behavior. Each step in the program had a double intent: to resist the child's violence and to foster a constructive fighting attitude. The implementation of each step of resistance was thus also an inner schooling.

Consider, for instance, the sit-in. The following instructions are handed out to the parents:

> One of the simplest and clearest manifestations of nonviolent resistance is the sit-in. This activity allows you to manifest parental presence without escalating or losing control. Its purpose is to convey to the child that you won't put up with his or her destructive acts anymore.
>
> Enter the child's room at a convenient time for you, when the child is in the room. Don't do this immediately in the wake of a display of aggressive behavior by the child, but a few hours or even a day later. This delay helps to prevent escalation ("Strike the iron while it is cold!"). Shut the door after you, and sit down in a way that prevents the child's leaving the room (e.g., the father sits before the door). After sitting down, say to the child: "We are not prepared to put up with this behavior anymore (describe specifically the unacceptable behavior). We are here to find a way to solve the problem. We will sit and wait until you suggest a solution." You should then remain quiet and wait for suggestions. If any are forthcoming, consider them positively. If the child answers you

with accusations ("It's my brother's fault!"), demands ("If you buy me a television set, I'll stop!"), or threats ("Then I'll run away from home!"), do not be provoked into an argument but continue sitting quietly. You may remark that what the child has said is not a solution, but by all means avoid being drawn into any discussion. All discussions carry a high risk of escalation.

Avoid blaming, sermonizing, threatening, or screaming. Wait patiently and do not be provoked into a verbal or physical struggle. Time, silence, and the fact that you remain in the room convey the message of parental presence.

If the child makes any positive suggestion (even a very small one), ask him a few clarifying questions in a positive spirit and then leave the room, saying that the suggestion will be given a chance. Do not question suspiciously the child's proposal. Do not threaten that you will return to sit in the room if the suggestion fails to materialize. If the child has already made the same suggestion in a previous sit-in, you may answer, "You've already made that suggestion and it didn't help. Now we need a suggestion that will work better!" If the child does not make a suggestion, stay in the room for 1 hour, then leave without any threat or warning that you will be back. When you leave, you can say, "We still haven't found a solution."

Points to remember:

(a) You must plan ahead the best time to sit in the room (you must have 1 hour free).

(b) You specifically indicate what you want, for example: "We are no longer willing to put up with your hitting your sister, calling her names, and ridiculing her." Very general or hazy goals are not helpful.

(c) If you anticipate that the child may respond with physical violence, it is advisable to have one or two other persons in the house (friends or relatives), but not in the room. In such a case, the child should be told, "Because we were afraid that you would be violent, we invited *X* to serve as a witness."

(d) If the child behaves violently despite the presence of the witnesses outside the room, you should ask them to enter the room. Experience with dozens of cases showed that the presence of a third party almost invariably stopped the violence.

(e) After the sit-in is over, the daily routine is to be continued without mentioning the sit-in or the desired change (Omer, 2004a).

This procedure is not only a potentially effective means of resistance but also an opportunity for countering the parents' destructive assumptions. The following typical interchanges illustrate some of the parents' assumptions and the therapist's possible rejoinders:

Parent: He's very manipulative and will propose something just to trick us out of the room!

Therapist: Any positive proposal indicates also a positive voice within him, even if a weak one, or even if he is not completely sincere. We want to strengthen this voice, instead of weakening it by ignoring it.

Parent: There isn't one chance in a thousand that she will make a proposal! And even less that she will really mean it!

Therapist: The goal of the sit-in is not to make her change, but to show that you are determined to resist.

Parent: (after the first sit-in) It didn't help at all! He feels he's won!

Therapist: You don't have to win, but only to persevere.

Parent: (after the sit-in) It didn't help! She did not change her behavior!

Therapist: Let us look at what you did at the sit-in; if you changed *your* behavior, this will help.

The constructive assumptions are conveyed not only by the therapist's answers, but by the very features of the sit-in: (a) Delaying the sit-in for a few hours after the violent occurrence helps the parents to free themselves from the immediacy principle and learn the value of low arousal in preventing escalation; (b) the sitting arrangement, with one of the parents blocking the exit, conveys the parents' determination to resist; (c) learning to stay quiet in the face of provocations is a good practice in the asymmetry of means; (d) accepting any positive suggestion by the child as legitimate strengthens the assumption of many-voicedness; (e) staying in the room for 1 hour reflects the assumption that the goal is not winning but persevering; and (f) bringing in external witnesses illustrates the use of publicity.

A central point is learning to view the sit-in not as a punishment but as a constructive display of resistance. Parents usually express their eagerness that the sit-in should work. The therapist may then say, "Don't expect quick results! The goal of the sit-in is to show that you decided to resist. Moreover, after a couple of sit-ins you will become tempered resistors." Thus, even a sit-in that the parents view as a downright failure is analyzed for its learning value. Actually, the sit-in can be viewed as successful if the parents agree to undertake another one (or another resistance step).

The addition of reconciliation gestures to the acts of actual resistance is especially designed to further the constructive fighting assumptions. The following are the instructions handed out to parents:

> Reconciliation gestures help to broaden your relationship with the child, so that it is no longer limited to the conflict between you. Research on escalation shows that the performance of such gestures reduces mutual aggression and improves the relationship. Reconciliation gestures are not a prize and they do not depend on the child's behavior. They allow you to express your love, while simultaneously carrying out nonviolent resistance. Reconciliation gestures do not replace nonviolent resistance but run parallel to it!
>
> Following are some main types of reconciliation gestures:
>
> (a) Statements, verbal or written, that express esteem and respect for the child, her talents, and her qualities. You can also express respect for her determination and fighting spirit. Don't fear that this would strengthen the child in the fight against you; on the contrary, by positively acknowledging the child's determination, you partly obviate her need to prove it.
>
> (b) Treats, such as food the child is especially fond of, or symbolic presents. It is important to be prepared for the child's refusal to accept the treat. In such case, limit yourselves to saying that you prepared the treat for her, but that she is free to take it or leave it. Treats should have no strings attached; the child decides how and if to accept them. Treats should never be expensive gifts (e.g., like a trip abroad) or something the child demands as a condition for improving his behavior. One treat with a special positive significance is to fix any of the child's belongings that the child broke in a fit of rage. Fixing the object then becomes a symbol for the desire to repair the relationship. Don't be afraid the child will view you as weak; your objective is not to look strong, but to demonstrate your presence as parents. Treats are a way to do so in a pleasant manner.
>
> (c) Suggesting a shared activity: You could suggest going on a hike, seeing a film, or participating in another shared activity that the child likes

and was perhaps used to doing with you in the past. Remember that she has the right to refuse without this being held against her.

(d) A special type of reconciliation gesture is expressing regret for your own violent reactions in the past. Some parents have reservations about this, fearing to be viewed as weak. Remember that reconciliation gestures are performed in parallel to nonviolent resistance. For this reason, a reconciliation gesture is never a token of submission but a positive gesture made out of choice.

It is very likely that at first, the child will reject your reconciliation gestures. This may simply indicate that your child is used to rejecting all your proposals indiscriminately or that she may fear that by accepting them he or she will appear weak. Reconciliations gestures, however, may help even when they are rejected, because they begin to restore parental presence in a positive way. Continue therefore with reconciliation gestures without forcing them on the child. In some cases, the child may outwardly reject your offer but give a silent token of acceptance. For instance, a child may refuse something the mother cooked for him, but the food item disappears from the fridge during the night. "Officially," the child has refused, but the food is already in his stomach, doing some productive work of reconciliation in there (Omer, 2004a).

Reconciliation counters the zero-sum mentality of destructive conflicts. In exercising reconciliation in parallel with resistance, the parents free themselves from the symmetry of retaliation. This release is abetted by the understanding that the child's refusal of the parents' reconciliation offers does not necessarily invalidate them. The parents' acceptance that all they can do is to change their own behavior weakens the hold of the illusion of control. Practice in reconciliation steps thus improves the parents' fighting assumptions on many counts.

Perhaps the most challenging of reconciliation steps for parents is the open expression of regret for past offenses. In so doing, the parents distance themselves from the "right–wrong," "weak–strong" and "lose–win" dichotomies that characterize demonic fighting. They also deepen their commitment to the asymmetry of means; they apologize without demanding an apology, or even without expecting that the child accept their apology. At times, this asymmetric step may have a quasi revolutionary impact.

A high-impact reconciliation procedure was developed for the parent-training project, on the basis of the Arab tradition of the *Sulkh* ('peace' or 'reconciliation' in Arabic; Jabbour, 1992). The *Sulkh* is an age-old ritual designed to prevent family feuds from degenerating into wars of vendetta.

The chances for an effective *Sulkh* are highest when one of the sides is willing to acknowledge responsibility one-sidedly, and make an asymmetric offer of compensation. The optimal start for the *Sulkh* is thus a one-sided retreat from an ideally balanced solution. No attempts are made to weigh the respective hurts; such an attempt would probably undermine the *Sulkh* attempt.

The traditional procedure begins with the nomination of a *Sulkh* committee, which is charged with conveying the *Sulkh* offer to the offended party, and conducting the negotiations between the sides. The *Sulkh* committee should be composed so as to have the best possible chances of being accepted by the offended party. Thus, community notables or members who are known to be especially respected by the offended family should be included. The very nomination of a *Sulkh* committee helps deactivate the strict honor code that characterizes family feuds. The committee approaches the injured side in a way stipulated by tradition, knocking at their door, and humbly asking to be accepted in a mediating role. The offer may be rejected, especially the first time it is made. The tradition then stipulates that the committee should come again the next day, and the day after it, repeating their request. Meanwhile, other mediators may step in, so as to persuade the family to accept the *Sulkh* committee. The family's acceptance of the committee is a crucial event. An Arab saying has it that "talking *Sulkh* is already *Sulkh*." Thus, in accepting the committee, the injured party tacitly pledges itself to refrain from any hostile acts throughout the period of negotiations. The negotiations are mediated by the committee from beginning to end. To prevent untoward events, any direct meetings between the parties are to be avoided during this stage. Tradition stipulates, for instance, that if a member of the offended family steps into a public vehicle in which a member of the offending family is sitting, the latter should step down. The negotiations deal with the form and contents of the public acknowledgment to be made by the offending family and the compensation that will be offered. When an agreement on these points is reached, the date for the *Sulkh* ceremony is set. The whole neighborhood is usually invited to participate, as well as people from other places. The gist of the ceremony is the public acknowledgment of responsibility by a leading member of the offending party, the handing over of the compensation (or of a written pledge to it), a ritualized hand-shaking, and a joint meal, where the leading members of the two parties eat at the same table. The tension grows to a pitch at the beginning of the ceremony, for it takes little to destroy the *Sulkh* before it is sealed. For this reason, each successful step is greeted by general jubilation. Sometimes when material compensation is offered, the offended party declares that it accepts the *Sulkh* without need for the payment. This is not an offensive step, but on the contrary, one that draws general acclaim. The public nature of the event is the strongest guarantee that the *Sulkh* will be kept. Members of both sides know that having recourse to violence after the *Sulkh* would involve general ostracism. The *Sulkh* embodies the readiness of a whole culture to relinquish its rigorous ideal of retributive justice in favor of a more charitable and tragic view of human fallibility. The following case presents our attempt to learn from this tradition and adapt the *Sulkh* to a thorny family problem.

CASE 17

George was 7 years old and Bob was 5 years old when their mother died. Their father, Burt, married again 5 years later. George had always been a highly impulsive and aggressive child. In the first 6 months after his father's marriage, George seemed to be developing a good relationship with Burt's wife, Joyce, although his overall level of aggressiveness remained high. Gradually, however, George began to view Joyce in a negative light, claiming she had usurped his rights and place in the house. One year after the marriage, he declared war against Joyce and said he would not stop until she left the house. This attitude worsened when Joyce got pregnant and gave birth to a son. George then tried to convince Bob that they were both being treated like Cinderella. Bob, who had a positive relationship with Joyce, was not convinced.

On a number of occasions, George destroyed Joyce's belongings and threw things at her. Once, when he threw a pointed stick at her, Joyce threw it back at him, scratching him on the neck. This was the only occasion in which Joyce reacted violently, but the event deteriorated the relationship even more. George became more violent, accused Joyce of being abusive, and threatened to go to the police. Burt took him to a psychiatrist, who tried to give him psychotherapy and medication. However, when the psychiatrist reacted critically to George's revenge plans against Joyce, George had a tantrum in the office, and overturned the psychiatrist's table. Burt had to be called in from the waiting room and pin George to the floor. The psychiatrist refused to treat George any longer. At this juncture, Burt and Joyce came to the parent-training project.

Following the program's guidelines, Burt conducted a number of sit-ins in George's room when George behaved violently toward Joyce. However, the only apparent effect of the sit-ins was to change the target of George's destructiveness; he now started destroying his own belongings, badly damaging the walls and door of his room. When a sit-in was conducted on this issue, George claimed that his father could not stop him from destroying his own property. The therapist proposed that Burt should go public about his nonviolent fight against George's violence, and involve a number of friends and relatives as helpers. The helpers came to a therapeutic session and were instructed on the principles of nonviolent resistance and on the importance of taking a clear stand against George's destructiveness. They should contact George whenever he had a violent outburst and tell him that they cared for him and loved him but would stand behind Burt in resisting George's destructive behavior. George's claim that it was his own property he was destroying met with the uniform reaction that destruction was destruction, no matter whose property was being destroyed. George told Burt defiantly that he would never give in. Burt said he knew full well that nothing could ever bring George to his knees. The helpers called George and repeated the message; they all agreed that George would never be defeated by force. They added, however, that it was their duty to help Burt resist the destruction. George raved and screamed, but the destructive bouts and the attacks gradually subsided. However, George declared again that he would never agree to live with Joyce in peace. He began avoiding the house, coming later and later in the evening. Sometimes he would stay out the whole night without telling his father where he was.

Similar problems appeared at school; George missed classes and played truant. A meeting at the school, in which the therapist, Burt, Joyce, and the school staff participated, led to a closer supervision over George in the school. This meting revealed that George had been joining a group of older kids who met at "the hut." This was an area that was viewed as "children's territory" by the school staff and the children alike. The hut had been erected by a group of teenagers at the farthest corner of the school's premises. It served as a meeting point for these kids during school breaks or when they wanted to stay out of class. Cigarette butts and an occasional beer can bore witness to the activities in the hut. The hut was tacitly tolerated by the school as a minor evil compared to the kids' leaving the premises altogether. Lately, however, the hut had begun attracting younger kids, and this constituted a breach in the unspoken agreement between the youngsters and the school. George's presence in the hut illustrated this new trend. The school direction agreed to the therapist's proposal that a program of regular visits from staff members to the hut would probably put an end to this negative development. In the visits, the staff members would require the kids to give over any illicit materials, and their parents would be notified. The staff also agreed with Burt that whenever something untoward happened, Burt should come to the school as soon as possible. This would signal to George that his father and the school were united in their efforts. An attempt was made to ask members of the student committee to join the program, by organizing home visits to George and by trying to involve him in joint activities. This, however, failed; the relationship between the school management and the student committee was too strained to allow for such a joint project. The staff members' visits to the hut had a positive result as far as the school was concerned; the hut became less and less frequented. No untoward substitute appeared to fill its place. However, the program failed to bring the expected results with George; his participation in the school activities did not rise. The school staff gradually assumed the view that George should be sent to a school for children with behavior problems. George told Burt he was willing to go to a boarding school, so as never to see Joyce again. He soon changed his mind, however, and said he would rather make life impossible to all than let Joyce win.

In a therapeutic session, Joyce said to the therapist that maybe she was to blame, and that if she had been more loving, things would surely be better. She thought she did not have the emotional resources to succeed with a traumatized child like George. She felt defeated and feared for the family's future. This seemed to the therapist an appropriate moment to introduce the idea of the *Sulkh.* The therapist said it was impossible to know how things might have turned out had Joyce been a different person. Perhaps even the warmest of stepmothers would have failed when faced with George's adamant rejection. Perhaps, however, something could be done to reduce the escalation and improve the atmosphere. The therapist described the procedure of the *Sulkh* and asked them whether they would be willing to undertake something in such a spirit. Specifically, the therapist asked Joyce whether she would be willing to make an open acknowledgment of the hurts that George had sustained from her in spite of her good intentions, and whether she would be ready to offer some kind of compensation. For instance, George's complaints that he had lost his place in the house could perhaps be addressed in a constructive way. Joyce was very willing; she felt she would not only be helping George, but also saving her marriage and her family. The therapist asked if there were any people that might come in question for a *Sulkh* committee. Joyce said there was a family that George often visited. The mother (Cheryl) had been a close friend of George's mother, and George would go to them on his own initiative, spending a lot of time particularly with the father (Ken) and with their 17-year-old son. In spite of Cheryl's critical view of Joyce (she blamed her for George's problems), Burt and Joyce were happy when George stayed with Cheryl's family, as this was probably the only positive influence to which he was exposed. Cheryl and Ken seemed a promising *Sulkh* committee. However, Joyce and Burt had doubts as to whether Cheryl would cooperate. The therapist proposed to put the question to a test. He invited the two couples to a joint meeting and explained the idea of the *Sulkh.* Cheryl reacted with skepticism, saying that George would not care for any such ritual. He needed love, and so long as did not get what he really needed, nothing would help. After this inauspicious beginning, Burt said that he and Joyce had thought of some practical solutions that might interest George. He brought up a plan of rebuilding their basement so as to include a room with a private entrance for George. In the future, Bob could join him in an adjoining room, thus creating an independent unit for the youngsters. This would show George that Joyce and Burt were willing to give him a real place in the house. Ken reacted positively to the whole proposal, saying that George might well like the idea of a public acknowledgment and apology by Joyce, especially about the event with the stick. Joyce said she was willing to do it. Ken and Cheryl agreed to feel George out about the possibility. Ken offered also to involve his son; he would talk to George about the advantages of a separate room with a private entrance. There was no need for this, however; George reacted with the greatest interest to the ideas of acknowledgment and compensation. At first, he said he wanted money as compensation, but was soon convinced that the separate room was a better idea. The negotiations extended for a number of weeks. George suddenly raised the demand that Joyce should acknowledge that she had hurt Bob as well. Cheryl supported this claim, but Joyce said she would not acknowledge something she did not feel was true. In a meeting between the couples, Burt told Cheryl that sticking to this demand would destroy the whole initiative. He invited her to talk with Bob about the matter if she so wished. Cheryl dropped the matter and George never mentioned it again.

The home atmosphere improved dramatically from the start of the negotiations. It proved true that "talking *Sulkh* is already *Sulkh.*" The change was so obvious that Joyce decided to make her acknowledgment without a formal ceremony; she told George in the presence of Burt and Bob that she knew she had hurt him and that her hitting him with the stick had been an act of violence. She said she wanted to make good on the hurts he had sustained by helping him design his room in the best possible way. George was pleased and the relations went on improving. Joyce was the one who explained the building plans to him and discussed the details with him.

However, a solution had still to be found to the problem with the school. Burt thought that George needed a strict school with very close supervision. He felt that with the improvement achieved by the *Sulkh*, an attempt could be made with less risk so that George would not view it as a punishment or banishment. A special day program for children with behavior problems answering Burt's requirements was found; it was probably the school with the strictest regime in the whole area. The result was very positive; George reacted well to the new blend of strictness at school and improved atmosphere at home. He declared daily that he hated the school; however, he went to school regularly, stopped skipping classes, and was not upset when he came home. The school director succeeded in coaching Burt on how to react to George's escapades by a clear regime of reward and punishment. Surprisingly (for the nonviolent resistance team), this worked quite well. But perhaps this regime would have been less successful, were it not for the atmospheric cleaning up achieved by the *Sulkh*.

Chapter **5**

The Tragic Wisdom of Consolation

Throughout the ages, consoling a person in pain has been viewed as a duty and a blessing. In the modern world, however, consolation has fallen into disrepute. Current expressions such as "cheap consolation" reflect its fallen value. Even the traditional formulas for consoling people in pain have become almost obsolete; one stammers the consolation awkwardly, if at all. Particularly puzzling is the fact that the skills of consolation find little place in the training of therapists. It is perhaps assumed that such skills cannot be taught or that they are irrelevant for the professional, because cure is the real business of therapy; or perhaps that the therapist steps in after the usual attempts at consolation have already failed. In any case, the proper realm of therapy is believed to lie over and beyond that of consolation. Consolation has thus become a forgotten wisdom.

Consolation, like its twin sister, acceptance, is a "tragic" virtue. The modern world with its ethos of control aims at solutions that leave no remnant. The tragic view, in contrast, has its starting point in the ubiquity of suffering. Where life is, suffering is, therefore all solutions must leave a remnant. The tragic outlook aims at the pursuit of a modicum of happiness in a miserable world; it is therefore acceptant and ameliorative, rather than curative. The hope of cure is uniquely directed at a stage where suffering is no more. Consolation, in contrast, is Janus-faced: One face is acceptant, the other encouraging. The first is oriented to the suffering, and the second to the possibility of reducing it. Suffering and loss are not eliminated; one moves ahead while looking back. The two sides of consolation are interdependent, as the readiness for amelioration usually entails relinquishing one's dreams of total recovery. Consolation is thus a bittersweet pill; it encourages in direct proportion to one's willingness to accept. There is only one kind of encouragement that involves no element of acceptance altogether: the positive-thinking kind that views every complaint as detrimental to the appropriate optimistic attitude. We believe that this kind of encouragement is not very encouraging. Being based on a rejection of the sufferer's right to suffer, it is often closer to condemnation than to consolation.

We consider consolation under three headings: the consoling relationship, loss, remembrance and consolation, and hope, disillusion, and consolation.

THE CONSOLING RELATIONSHIP

Interestingly, consolation is usually extended to a person who seems and probably feels unconsolable. It thus may look like an impossible task; one speaks of overcoming a loss to someone for whom the loss is all. Therefore the effects of consolation are commonly unnoticeable; one offers consolation and the sufferer remains apparently unconsolable. One knows that even then, consolation may gradually seep in, but between the act of offering it and the slowly evolving consolatory process, there is no obvious relation of cause and effect. The consoler should thus assume that many factors come into play in this process and that the consoling act is but one among many.

Consolation must therefore be offered in full awareness of its humble significance. It can be offered, but not pushed. Any attempt to press the sufferer to accept it would be self-defeating. The readiness to be consoled may or may not evolve, according to the legitimate needs of the sufferer. Jacob, in the Bible story, refused to be consoled over the loss of Joseph. It would be absurd to argue he was "wallowing in misery" or displaying "pathological grief." If someone temporarily succeeded in selling him the idea that he should stop grieving, Jacob might feel he had been guilty of the grossest self-betrayal. The anger the sufferer sometimes expresses at the consoler is thus quite understandable, for in consoling one often implies that the sufferer should walk the path of renunciation. It is then as if he was being denied the right to protest against fate and resist fate's cruel dictate.

Rushing the sufferer is a tactless but common mistake that is often committed without awareness. A woman client with a potentially fatal illness asked for help with trouble falling asleep. The therapist (one of the authors) tried to help her with relaxation training. When, after a few sessions, she seemed to be already sleeping better, the therapist told her he thought they were finished. On hearing this, she picked up her bag, wrote her check without a word, and left in anger. She had rightly perceived that the therapist's impatience was due to the anxiety her condition evoked in him. The therapist felt he had been guilty of the grossest lack of empathy, a feeling that became stronger when she died 6 months later.

The "rushing" comforter conveys a message of wishing to avoid contact with the sufferer, as if out of fear of contagion. The late Marianne Amir, when ill with terminal cancer, wrote an article entitled "Run For Your Life!," describing the impact of this avoidant attitude on the sufferer. One of her friends would call at times she knew she was not at home and leave a message saying, "I wanted to know how you are feeling, but I did not want to disturb. No need to call back." Another friend left a bouquet of flowers at the door. A third would shorten all contacts as much as possible, ending them with a cheerful, "All will be well!!" Perhaps the most unhelpful of all "encouraging" attitudes was that of colleagues who found fault with her sadness and her attitude toward the illness, saying she was not really helping herself get better (Amir & Kalemkerian, 2003). The difficulty that friends, colleagues, and doctors experience in such situations is understandable; they feel helpless, anxious, and overwhelmed. It remains true, however, that a person who displays such an attitude cannot console.

The impatience conveyed by the rushing consoler reflects another aspect of the consoling relationship; whether the giver feels similar to or different from the sufferer. The impatient helper conveys a message of difference: "We are not in the same boat; you are heading that way and I am heading this way!" No wonder the sufferer feels abandoned. A potentially helpful consolation attempt conveys a message, not only of closeness, but also of basic similarity, "This could happen to me, too!" Of course such a message does not have to be made explicit, but is implied in the consoler's attitude.

In the short story, "Misery," by Chekhov (1979), a coachman who has just lost his only son waits for clients under the falling snow. He and his horse are gradually covered in white. Throughout the story, he unavailingly tries to tell his passengers about his child's death. They interrupt him with gruff commands or loud complaints about other drivers or pedestrians. One of the patrons cuts him short, gruffly saying "We shall all die!" At the end of the story, the coachman remains alone with his horse. Unable to bear his pain alone any longer, he starts telling the horse about it. To make matters clear for the horse, he asks it to imagine it had a foal that suddenly died, would not that be painful? A similar insight into the nature of consolation is one of the themes of Tolstoy's novel, *The Death of Ivan Illyitch* (2003). The dying Ivan is surrounded by people who keep telling him he will get well and avoid by all means any talk of illness or death. The servant, Gerasim, is the only one who never lies to him. When Ivan feels pains in his legs, Gerasim sits all night long by his bed, with Ivan's feet on his shoulders. Ivan asks him if sitting for so long is not too hard on him and Gerasim tells him it is nothing, for "We shall all die!" Gerasim's answer is the same as that of the gruff patron in Chekhov's story. However, the compassionate, nonevasive, and patient attitude of Gerasim makes his consoling message, "We shall all die!" acceptable and helpful. The assumption of similarity lies at the root of the consolatory interaction. Thus the coachman in Chekhov's story draws consolation from telling the horse about how it would feel to lose its only foal.

Consolation thus involves a lowering of the barriers between giver and receiver. The boundaries of individuality are thinned out and the giver becomes also a receiver, as a reflection of the consolation offered. Consolation and its twin-feeling, compassion, bring to the fore not only the basic similarity but also the interconnectedness between the parties. In the Buddhist tradition, this is illustrated by the image that compassion is not experienced toward another that is totally separate from oneself, but is rather like the attitude of the mouth toward the ailing stomach; the mouth knows full well that it does not stand apart from the ailing stomach, so that in "being compassionate" toward it, it is actually "being compassionate" to itself.

This feeling that the compassionate participant is also a receiver is made manifest in the feelings of awe that tragedy arouses in those that witness it, in real life or in art. As a respectful witness of a human tragedy, one feels humbled, but often also spiritually uplifted. One is humbled by the extent of the suffering and uplifted through compassion and participation in the other's humanity in the face of an overwhelming fate. Such is the purifying experience of *catharsis* that, in the view of Aristotle, constitutes the therapeutic effect of tragic drama on the viewer.

CASE 19

Albert had been horribly struck by fate. Ten years after his eldest son died of cancer, his daughter was killed in a terrorist attack. His broken-hearted wife died 6 months later. Albert had still another son and two grandchildren left, with whom he maintained a warm relationship. He had retired from work a few years previously, so he found little reason to go out. He stopped leaving the house and spent most of his days mourning over his losses. A number of reaching-out attempts were made by a community social worker, but she found it impossible to overcome Albert's barrier of grief. A proposal to have Albert sent to a psychiatrist was rejected by him immediately. One more attempt was made by a therapist who offered him a trial of five sessions to see if they could work together. Albert came punctually to the sessions and it seemed that a good therapeutic alliance was developing. The therapist was positively surprised by Albert's sober and dignified behavior. This seemed to point to inner strengths that might help him overcome his condition. At the end of the fifth session, however, Albert surprised the therapist by telling her that although he was grateful for the therapeutic attempt, there was no point in continuing. The therapist phoned him a number of times, but all her attempts to renew the therapy were politely declined. The therapist sent Albert the following letter, 3 months after the last contact between the two:

> Dear Albert,
>
> Although we have not met for awhile, I wanted to tell you that I think about you often. Meeting you, a man who was so awfully struck by fate, was a meaningful event for me. In our sessions, you told me of the three chapters in your life: the hard chapter of your childhood, with the ugly fights between your parents; the happy chapter of your marriage, your involved fatherhood, and your successful professional career; and the shattering chapter, in which all the gifts that life had given you were taken away: you lost one son, then a daughter, and then your loving wife. You were bereft three times in a row. Fate has been incredibly cruel to you. As in the story of Job in the Bible, one listens and simply cannot believe.
>
> I wanted to tell you not only that I acknowledge your endless tragedy, but also that I view your life decisions as perfectly legitimate; you have decided to spend the years that are left to you in mourning over your losses and in a quiet maintenance of your relationship with your son and grandchildren. I find it legitimate and reasonable that you say, "Don't offer me psychiatric treatment, I am not a medical case." Your story reminds me of the story of Jacob, who lost his beloved Rachel, and who was then told that also Joseph, his dearest son, had died. Jacob, like you, "refused to be consoled." All that happened in your life happened cruelly, without rhyme or reason. You know that no positive change is in the offing. I am writing you to express my respect for your endless pain and for the dignified way in which you bear it. With your permission, I will phone you in a couple of weeks, not to offer you therapy, but only to get in touch with you and ask you how you are feeling.

When the therapist called 3 weeks later, Albert was warm and positive. He said that nobody had ever told him that what he did was right, and that he was deeply grateful to the therapist for it.

LOSS, REMEMBRANCE AND CONSOLATION

Human beings are perhaps unique in the way they undergo loss, because they are able to preserve in memory the experience of what was lost. Memory makes loss both more acute and more bearable; more acute, because it postpones the balming effects of forgetfulness; more bearable, because in memory, a valuable remnant escapes the totality of the loss. The consolatory use of remembrance is present in all cultures. The 19th century cultural historian, Fustel de Coulanges described in his masterpiece *The Ancient City* how, in many societies, the institutionalized remembrance of the group's common ancestors served as a basic tie for the extended family, the clan, the tribe, the city, and the nation (Fustel de Coulanges, 1864/1980). The hearth, in which a permanent fire kept alive the memory (and to the antique mind, also the living souls) of the ancestors, was both the spiritual and the physical center of the group. So long as the hearth existed and the fire burned, the links with the ancestors and between the members of the community were preserved. Forgetting to keep the fire alight or neglecting it in favor of the more practical business of life was a betrayal of the ancestors, the self, and the group. Exile was the worst imaginable disaster because it signified disconnection from the living fire, or worse, its extinction. As the family grew into the clan, and the clan into the tribe, the family hearth turned into a temple. The temple was the heart of the community and the center of joint remembrance. Obliterating any element of the temple service was sacrilegious. On festive days, the community came alive in its togetherness by rites of unification and celebration of the joint ancestors; anyone who absented himself from these rites had as much as cut himself off from the community. One might venture the hypothesis that the acceptance and transcendence of loss that is embodied in such remembrance rites is essential to humanity as such.

For instance, in the Jewish mourning tradition, a series of ordinances, both private and communal, provide the bereaved with a context for relating with the dead and with a support system that validates this relationship. The bereaved is enjoined to mourn and to remember, but a clear limit is set on the extent of his mourning. Tradition stipulates what the mourning acts should be and how the bereaved should gradually withdraw from them. Each step in the mourning process is marked by a communal event. In the Talmud, the exact length of each mourning stage is specified: The first 3 days are devoted to crying, the first 7 days to intensive grieving, and the first month to a gradual return to normal duties. Throughout the first year, the mourner takes upon himself a series of limitations that express sadness and remembrance. After this period, special prayers and memorial days are stipulated, extending for the whole life of the bereaved. The individual mourner who would go on grieving in ways that go beyond these limits is admonished by God: "You should not be more merciful than I am!" (*Babylonian Talmud: Moed Katan*, p. 26b). The work of mourning is the business, not only of the bereaved, but of the whole community. The community's participation endows the mourning of the individual with supraindividual meaning, setting upon it the seal of cultural validation. The group also helps the bereaved to maintain and crystallize the memory of the dead by a process of intensive dialogue. The communal aspect of the individual loss is highlighted, for instance, in the daily prayer, where the community says to the mourner: "God will comfort you *together with all those that mourn over Zion and Jerusalem*" (emphasis added). The holiday prayer of "remembrance for the souls of the dead" (*Hazkarat-Neshamot*) solemnly magnifies and contextualizes the individual's suffering, linking it to the historical losses of the Jewish people throughout the ages. There is a cyclic ordering of mourning events around the year. Mourning thus becomes a recurrent occurrence with a place in the normal calendar. This ritualized process regulates also the relationship between the bereaved and the departed. This relationship is based on the assumption that the souls of the dead live on in the hands of God, fulfilling a crucial role as advocates and helpers for the living.

This ritualization of the mourning process has a deep consolatory value; it endows the process with individual and supraindividual meaning, specifies activities that redefine and preserve the relationship with the dead, and enables a culturally validated return to normal life. Perhaps the phenomenon that is termed, *pathological grief*, can be explained by the waning of such mourning traditions in the modern world. In this view, the person suffering from pathological grief might actually be suffering from the lack of established ways for keeping in touch with the dead. Without such culturally validated ways, the individual might experience the act of remembrance as weak and hollow. A communal echo is lacking that would allow the mourner to feel he was remembering well. Encouragement by the people in his entourage to the effect that he was grieving for too long and should go ahead with the business of living might then leave the mourner in an even deeper vacuum.

This analysis suggests that therapeutic attempts that aim at helping the pathological mourner to complete the work of separation might be misguided. Michael White described how clients who are diagnosed as suffering from "delayed mourning" or "pathological grief" are often expected to achieve separation by *grief work*; this is a normative process in which the mourner goes through a series of well-defined stages that culminate in "a fully experienced 'goodbye,' (an) acceptance of the permanence of the loss of the loved one, and a desire to get on with a new life that is disconnected from that person." (White, 1989, p. 29). White argued that a therapeutic dialogue that is oriented by this "goodbye metaphor" could aggravate the sense of emptiness, worthlessness, and loss of self that these clients experience. He proposed instead to help these people reclaim the inner dialogue with the departed. He substituted the goodbye metaphor by the metaphor of "saying hello again," and developed a series of therapeutic questions to reorient the mourner in this direction: "If you were seeing yourself through your mother's eyes right now, what would you be noticing about yourself that you could appreciate?" "How did she know these things about you?" "What is it about you that told her about this?" "What qualities in yourself are you awakened to when you bring alive the enjoyable things that your mother knew about you?" "How can you let others know of these qualities that were clearly visible to her?" White also helps the mourner to put these questions in a communal context by having them be discussed and validated in the presence of friends and relatives. This kind of therapeutic work could perhaps be seen as an attempt to partially fill in the vacuum left by the waning of mourning traditions.

HOPE, DISILLUSION AND CONSOLATION

The consoling effect of any message is a function of cultural context and life situation. The idea of heaven, for instance, can be comforting in some contexts, but be experienced as an evasive attempt at cheap consolation in other contexts. In a poignant observation recorded in the diary of a German officer at the time of the mass executions of Jews by SS squads in Eastern Europe, mention is made of a father who talks softly to his young daughter and points to heaven before both are shot (Hilberg, 2003). Even if in a different situation, thoughts of heaven might perhaps have been of little comfort for this man, the total closeness to his daughter before death and his ability to say something to ease her pain, might have made the message consoling for him no less than for her.

In what follows, we do not attempt to do justice to the variety and richness of consolation themes, but focus on a few that are most significant to us. In the themes we will be broaching, consolation entails a *work of disillusion* that is typical of the tragic position. This work of disillusion may be directed either at an illusion of total hope or an illusion of total suffering. The two usually go hand in hand: images of total suffering tend to engender pictures of total hope, and vice versa. The tragic attitude aims at dispelling both. The helper, of course, should be wary of pushing the sufferer along the path of disillusion. As already mentioned, consolation cannot be forced; however, the seeds of disillusion that arise spontaneously in the sufferer can be "watered" to bring out sprouts of consolation.

Mind-Over-Body Illusion

The fear of bodily suffering is such a compelling and universal experience that the market value of a new book can often be predicted from the extent of bodily immunity it promises. Thus, books of popular psychology that sell the idea of mind over body often reach a very wide circulation. The widening application of the term, *psychosomatic* to ever-new diseases reflects the attempt to annex terrain traditionally belonging to the bodily sphere into the more influenceable psychological one, a phenomenon that Szasz (1974) termed *psychoimperialism.* Viewing a physical disease as due to a psychological cause is doubly appealing, for the suffering is made understandable and the hopes of cure are raised. In contrast, viewing a disease as strictly physical (or worse, as genetic) makes it morally unaccountable and potentially incurable. An even deeper betrayal of the hopes of mind over body is giving back to the "physicalists" territory that belongs by rights to the "mentalists," for example, agreeing to the presence of biological factors in mental disease.

The tendency to subordinate the physical to the psychological can be manifested in different forms, such as the widespread inclination to view bodily symptoms as psychological, the psychodemonic belief that a person developing a disease somehow "wanted it to happen," or the hope that psychological treatments for all illnesses may be found. Perhaps the most extreme mind-over-body belief on the market is the doctrine of physical immortality, according to which the right mental attitude could postpone death for ever. The mind-over-body attitude often leads to a blaming stance toward the diseased person who "fails to improve." In a case we have reported elsewhere (Omer & Alon, 1997), the previously supportive family of a woman with terminal cancer developed a highly critical attitude toward her when, against the dictates of her healer, she decided to take analgesics to ease her pain.

Many assume that telling a client with a psychological problem that it has physical roots or that he needs medical treatment must be a great disappointment. In effect, some disappointment may well arise, for the message runs counter to the client's hopes. Moreover, "physical" seems worse than "psychological," and the client may feel his case is worse than he or she had previously thought. The disappointment, however, may also bring relief. The French philosopher, Alain, tells the following story:

> Some time ago, I met a friend who was suffering from a kidney stone and was in a very somber mood. Everyone knows that this kind of illness causes sadness. As I mentioned this to him, he immediately agreed. I then concluded: "Knowing that this illness causes sadness, you should not be surprised that you are sad, nor be depressed by the fact." This reasoning made him laugh. No mean achievement for someone with a kidney stone (Alain, 1928/1985, p. 20).[1]

The relief experienced by a person who is told that her suffering has a physical rather than a psychological cause has various sources. First, saying that the suffering is psychological makes our nature responsible for it; the

[1]Our translation. The page numbers are from the Folio (Alain 1985) edition.

suffering is then rooted in our whole being rather than in a specific organ. In contrast, saying that it has a physical cause circumscribes it. To quote Alain again: "Everything with us is alright, except for the suffering" (1928/1985, p. 22). This is true also for our bad moods: "It is my body that is arguing: these opinions come from the stomach" (1928/1985, p. 24). Thereby not only our sense of guilt is reduced, but also the additional suffering that stems from our attempts to stop the bad mood by sheer willpower. Alain compares this extra suffering to that of a person who worsens a cough by forcefully trying to get rid of it. Upon viewing someone who unwittingly makes her own suffering worse by chafing or complaining, external observers are often led to assume a masochistic or self-destructive intent. Alain disabuses us of this view: "Sometimes we believe to see in others a kind of attraction to misery ... from which we conclude that some mystical and at the same time diabolical feeling may be at work. This is only our imagination. There is no such depth in a man that scratches himself" (1928/1985, p. 32). Another reason for the experience of relief has to do with the sufferer's relation to others. So long as the pain is attributed to psychological causes, others may expect the sufferer to triumph over it by an appropriate mental attitude. Inability to do so is then viewed as a sign of irrationality, ill will, or lack of consideration. The attribution of a physical cause may therefore contribute not only to making the pain legitimate in the individual's own eyes, but also in the eyes of others; they are less angry at him, and the relationship improves.

All these paths to relief are often witnessed in clinical practice. The depressed client who is told his depression is probably due to an inborn tendency is relieved from his burden of guilt and obligation to defeat an enemy that remains stubbornly out of reach. Sometimes, his self-accusations and fruitless attempts to drive the depression away by sheer willpower evaporate. Similarly, the obsessive-compulsive client who is told the obsessive ideations, being linked to a chemical dysfunction, will occasionally arise no matter what he or she does to prevent them, learns that his or her best option is not to aggravate them by fruitless attempts at suppression, but to let them come and go, like bad weather (Hayes, et al., 2000).

The acceptance of a physical core does not entail a passive attitude. The snowball metaphor, for instance, may open a variety of paths for ameliorative action. So long as there are only two mutually exclusive options, "physical" *or* "psychological," much energy is wasted in the tug-of-war between the two. Assuming that a physical core is present allows one to focus on the snowball's removable layers. Interestingly, the snowball metaphor can help mitigate not only the damages of the mind over body, but also those of the body-over-mind illusion. In one case, a man who had suffered for many years from bouts of violent behavior was diagnosed as suffering from a small and probably benign brain tumor. The surgeon, who was a staunch upholder of the body-over-mind position, aroused high hopes that removal of the tumor would eliminate the outbursts. The therapist told the client and his family that it might be wiser not to expect the outbursts to stop completely after the operation, because habits of thinking, feeling, and relating had slowly developed that would not just go away with the tumor's excision. The tumor was successfully removed. The violent bouts were reduced, but were far from disappearing. The therapist's preparation of the client and his family for this eventuality contributed much to their ability to cope with this disappointment. In the course of 2 years, a new adaptation evolved, the aggressive episodes were further reduced, and the client became free of total hopelessness as well as of total hopes.

People find it especially hard to consider biological factors in the explanation of children's violent behavior. Such an explanation is viewed as stigmatic for the child and as an attempt to let the real guilty parties (usually the parents) off the hook. Moreover, agreeing to a physical cause might legitimize the fatalistic attitude, "It is genetic, so nothing can be done!" In our opinion, both arguments are false; there is no stigma in saying that some children are born with a lower reaction threshold and attention span, a tendency to stronger emotional reactions, less sensitivity to pain, and a more restless temperament. There is little doubt that these characteristics, which have been linked to a high risk for the development of violent behaviors, have a biological core (Bates, Petit, Dodge, & Ridge, 1998; Moffit, 1990; Moffit & Henry, 1991). Understanding that these children have special needs because of their biological characteristics leads to a greater readiness to invest efforts rather than the opposite. In our experience, informing the parents of an aggressive child about biological factors tends to make them more motivated and involved (Omer, 2004a). However, in spite of the accumulating knowledge, the contention that there is a physical component in the development of children's aggressive behavior is still viewed as the epitome of political incorrectness. This may well be because such an imputation would spoil the angelic view of the child and the utopian hope that all would be well if only the child were let free to flourish.

The inescapability of bodily decay is the starting point of many tragic philosophies. In the Buddha legend, it was prophesied that prince Gautama (who later became the Buddha) would grow to be either the greatest of kings or the greatest of spiritual masters. However, according to the prophecy, he would only become a king if he were kept in total innocence of aging, illness, and death. To tip the scale in favor of the kingly option, his father built Gautama a palace totally isolated from its surroundings and with all imaginable pleasures for body and mind. The prince grew up happily with no inkling of suffering. However, he wished to see the world and, against his father's command, prevailed on his servant to take him out on a ride in a carriage. They secretly left by the northern gate. Some distance away from the palace the prince saw a man who was different from everyone he had ever seen; he walked bent over, leant on a staff, his face was wrinkled, and he had no hair. He asked the servant who was this man, if he was a man at all. The servant answered it was an old man. The prince asked how do old men arise, and the servant answered that all become old, if they live long enough. The prince went back to the palace deep in thought. A few days later, he asked to be taken out again. They left by the southern gate and some distance away, the prince saw an even stranger creature; its body had big white stains and its face was disfigured. He asked the servant who was this man, if he was a man at all. The servant answered it was a sick man—a leper. The prince asked how do sick men arise, and the servant answered that all become sick, if they live long enough. The prince, by now deeply perplexed, returned to the palace. A few days later he asked to be taken out again. They left in another direction, and the prince saw a man that looked asleep, and yet was not really asleep, for some people were carrying him and his skin had a strange color. The prince asked what was this man, and the servant answered it was a dead man, and that all would die, after they had lived their life. The prince was in total shock. Three horrible truths had been disclosed to him; the inevitability of aging, illness, and death. The prince went out a fourth time, and saw a man who was almost naked, had no possessions, and yet his face was filled with peace. He asked who this was. He was told it was a "sadhu-mendicant," who had given up his worldly goods and devoted his life to the search for truth. The prince decided to give up all his goods and to strike out into the wilderness to solve the riddle of suffering and happiness. The acceptance of the ubiquity of suffering turned him into one of the greatest consoling masters of all ages.

Illusions of Unbearable Suffering

Human beings are endowed with the capacity of creating not only positive illusions, but also fantasies of a horrible future. Many people suffer great anguish from possible images of unbearable pain. Constant worrying and fearing for the future can cause deep unhappiness. Attempts to dispel the anguish by pointing to the low probability of the feared events are notoriously ineffective. The stoic philosophers have opted for a different consoling approach; they guide us in a meditation about the nature of time that may help us achieve some freedom from the oppressive sense of an agonizing imminent future.

These philosophers teach that neither the past nor the future can harm us, because the past no longer exists and the future does not yet exist. Past and future exist only when we think about them. Of course, we think about them very much, and work hard at the mental construction of fears and regrets. Alain, the modern stoic, compares us to a juggler who manages to hold a large number of very sharp knives in a shaky equilibrium on his nose; they make out a kind of frightening tree that he keeps from falling by agonizing little jerks of his body. Like this juggler, we are imprudent artists who keep all of our regrets and fears gingerly poised on our heads (Alain, 1928/1985). The practical question is how to stop this foolish juggling.

Surprisingly, even highly anxious people often experience calmness, when they are beset by real tribulations. Imre Kerstesz (1992), the Nobel prize-winning author of *Fateless*, described how, upon his return from the concentration camps, he was asked by a journalist to report about his stay in hell. Kertesz, who was then 16, said he could not say much about hell, because he had had no experience of it. If he could at all conceive of hell, he would imagine it as a place where suffering was so intense that one could not be bored, but even in Auschwitz, he had experienced boredom. When asked how he had been able to endure, he answered, "Time helped." Time, he said, made one live through things one step at a time. Going to a camp began with a railway station, not exactly luxurious, but bearable. Things then happened one by one, and one always had only this one thing to bear. Understanding came slowly, and one was always busy trying to meet the immediate demands. As one finished with one thing, one was already busy with the next. Even while standing on the line before the Auschwitz doctor who sent people to the right or to the left, he had been busy with his place in the line, perhaps getting angry that it was too slow, or that someone was shoving him from behind. Had this sequence in time not existed and had the whole experience fallen on him at once, he could never have withstood it. And yet he had met inmates who had been in the camp for 4, 6 or even 12 years. In order to be still there, these people had had to get past these 4, 6 or 12 years, that is, 4, 6 or 12 times 365 days, multiplied by 24 hours, multiplied by so many minutes and seconds. Precisely this passage of unthinkable time had made it possible for them to bear it, for they had to go through it a moment at a time, ever busy with each moment.

This description is true also for less immense kinds of suffering. Consider, for instance, how often healthy people say about chemotherapy: "I could not bear it! I cannot bear to be nauseous!" And yet, very few people refuse chemotherapy because of nausea. When one gets there, one goes through the nausea, one moment at a time. The idea of chemotherapy as one endless, nauseous experience seems unbearable, but the actual experience is not chemotherapy, but one moment at a time. The illusion that the suffering is unbearable has to do with our projecting the whole idea of what has to be gone through (e.g., the hell of concentration camp or chemotherapy) into one single imaginary moment.

There is an additional mistaken projection in our illusions of future suffering: We imagine that the person we are now is the same person who will have to endure what we now cannot see ourselves as enduring. We imagine that it is this "I–now" who will have to experience this unimaginable trauma. We forget that this I–now will perforce become a whole series of I–nows, who may face their tribulations with a wholly different mind. The same reasoning may help us with the fear that we cannot bear to die. It is not the I–now that will die at all; this I–now, presently alive and kicking, cannot accept the transition into extinction. However, the other I–nows that we will become eventually may soften up a bit. As a wise person put it, "It is not the living that die, but the dying."

CASE 20

Andre was a businessman who found himself undergoing financial pressure. It became more and more difficult to refinance his many projects and the threat of bankruptcy hovered over his head. He had initially come for help with his sleep problem (he wanted to stop taking sleeping pills), his bodily condition, and his excessive weight. These goals, however, receded into the background as the pressure grew. He then began thinking that, as long as the situation remained acute, he had no energy left for these goals. He started to come only occasionally for therapy, so as to get some immediate relief when the pressure became too strong. He said that only when the immediate crisis was over would he be able to dedicate himself to the pursuit of more far-sighted goals. The crisis however stayed on, and Andre found himself running faster and faster in order to stay in the same place. He came to the therapist again after an interruption of a few months, when he awoke from a dream in which he was dressed in rags and was looking for a place for him and his family to live in a slum. He told the therapist he believed he had been dreaming this dream every night, but usually forgot it on awakening. He was worried that the dream's bursting upon his consciousness might signal he was becoming more pessimistic and might be nearing the breaking point.

Andre: I have to overcome my defeatism! I must find the energy for a final spurt!

Therapist: Maybe we should look for ways to help you endure better.

Andre: I don't believe I have much strength left to endure. No one can endure this kind of pressure for long.

Therapist: Do you remember when you first felt the need to find the energy for a final spurt?

Andre (laughing): About 5 years ago.

Therapist: What would you have thought then, had you been told that after 5 years you would still be fighting bankruptcy?

Andre: I would have gone crazy!

Therapist: We usually don't know how much we can endure. Perhaps becoming more aware of how much you can endure and how to do it would be a better goal than finding the energy for a final spurt.

Andre: I fear this dream shows that I am near the end.

Therapist: Perhaps not. Perhaps it shows you are preparing yourself to endure far more than you usually think possible.

The therapist told Andre about the passage in Kertesz's book about how life in the concentration camp was lived from one moment to the next. Andre remarked that many people he knew were currently making the discovery that they could bear the unbearable. Maybe the era of relative security in which he and the therapist had lived most of their lives might be nearing its end; the economic crisis and political terror were shattering it. The conversation than veered to the fact that throughout history, people had always endured the utmost in insecurity. The therapist's and Andre's parents were cases in point. How had they managed? Perhaps our generation had been "spoiled" by an illusory security?

Andre: If we have been programmed by evolution to withstand insecurity, 50 years of illusory security could not wipe this out! (laughing). Perhaps my dream shows that I am readying myself to be a caveman again!

At the end of the session, Andre decided to involve his daughter (whom he had kept in the dark about the financial situation, so as to save her unnecessary pain) in all particulars of his business. The daughter became a source of real support for Andre. A few days after the session, Andre called the therapist and said that, because the difficulties might well stay on for another 5 years, he should perhaps start caring about his physical fitness and his weight problem. This good intention proved short-lived. Yet, Andre's attitude seemed to be changing to the "constructive pessimism" of a long-distance runner.

Illusions of Hope[2]

The tragic outlook may be unpalatable to many because it is seen as furthering pessimism and as undermining hope. Hope is vital for existence. It is notorious that the inmates of prisoner camps would often die not of lack of

[2]This section follows closely on Omer & Rosenbaum (1997). We are thankful to R. Rosenbaum for allowing us to use this material.

food, but of lack of hope. At the entrance to Dante's Hell stands written: "Give up all hope you who enter!" Hopelessness is thus the very essence of hell. However, there is also a downside to hope. The "singing-tomorrows" of totalitarian utopias either of the left or of the right have engendered horrors that were no less frightful than those of Dante's Hell.

In its rigid forms, hope has victims not only in the social, but also in the individual sphere. Examples like the following are not rare:

> (a) a concert pianist had once achieved a very high level of playing. After months of pitiless self-drilling, she had played for 2 months like an angel. However, just as it had come, her newfound agility left her. In the beginning, she was sure she would get it back. She stepped up her self-demands and refused to ease off despite the onset of wrist and shoulder pains. She gradually became a prisoner of her hope, until playing became totally impossible because of chronic muscular spasm.
>
> (b) a man came to therapy because his wife was physically abusive. She would periodically attack him with fists, nails, and whatever object came to her hand. However, he hoped his love and patience would prevail over her anger. After an interruption of a few months he came back to therapy and told that he had been in the hospital. His wife had taken a large kitchen knife and plunged it between his ribs. He had been recovering from the attack ever since. Once again, he raised the issue of how the relationship now had a real chance of improving. His therapist was dumbfounded: "I don't understand. How can you stay with this woman, after she's stuck a knife in you?" The client answered: "Well, she didn't hit anything vital."
>
> (c) A father of three children found himself in a dilemma about his marriage. He and his wife were excellent friends and a good parent team. However, he felt no romantic attachment toward her. He had a vivid image of how love could energize his life. He knew it would probably take him years to find his dream of love, for he was not an emotionally expansive person. The very possibility of finding love, however, drained his marriage of value. He ended by leaving.

These peoples' hopes had arguably rigidified into what we may term a "hope disease." The hopes were not necessarily illusory, for the pianist might perhaps recover his skill, the abusive wife overcome her aggressiveness, and the disappointed husband find romantic love. The panegyrics of hope are filled with such tales. The merits of hope are often viewed as highest precisely when its objects seem most unattainable. Hope would not be so seductive if it could only be placed on easy objects. And yet, something must be wrong in the way these people became slaves to a hope that caused them and their near ones so much suffering.

Whether a hope turns into a "hope disease" is not only a question of how realizable it is. Hope can be diseased in itself, in its very process and mechanism, when it: (a) leads to a disparaging attitude toward the present, (b) leads to an all-out fight with no room for sacrifices, and (c) attempts to stamp out any alternative state of mind. A rigid hope thus presents a mirror image of a demonic attitude: It is the vision of the perfect condition that should follow upon the extirpation of the demon.

Many thinkers in the past have pointed out these dangers. For instance, that hope often goes hand in hand with fear and disappointment. Thus, according to Spinoza, "There is no hope without fear neither fear without hope" (*Ethics*, part III, explication of definition 13). Similarly, a quotation that is attributed to Bernard Shaw that "There are two catastrophes in life: the first is when our dreams are not fulfilled: the second, when they are." Interestingly, it is precisely the hopeful person who carries a shade of disappointment within the very heart of her hope that may best succeed in keeping hope nondiseased; knowing that fate can turn her hopes to naught, she manages not to be blinded by them. It is as if the inner readiness to be disappointed worked as an anticipatory consolation.

Hope becomes diseased when it makes one grasp at phantoms. One hates one's actual life, believing that all will be well if only certain things happen. Ironically, the higher one's hopes, the less they satisfy, even when the desired goals seem to be attained. The disappointed hoper then argues with his disappointment, saying that it is merely due to the incomplete possession of the objects, persons, or situations that he views as essential to bliss. He then keeps striving for fuller possession, ever tantalized by the image of a satisfaction that lies just around the corner. Meanwhile, one misses what is there. Thus, as Pascal states: "We never live but expect to live. We are never happy, because we are always readying ourselves for our future happiness" (Pascal, *Thoughts*, #47).

The enthusiasts of positive thinking would object that the readiness to be disappointed cannot but diminish the zest for decisive action. We find this objection pointless. The refusal to be duped by an idealized future vision does not at all restrain acting; on the contrary, one acts more flexibly. This agrees well with the tragic ideal; one strives for the better, knowing that not all depends on one's strivings. This ideal was illustrated by the attitude of the nondemonic resistor: "I cannot make you do what I want! I can only do my part!" The same is true for any personal goal whatsoever; the end result always depends on the confluence of factors that we poetically term *fate*.

Comte-Sponville (1984) observed that we hope for an ideal future because we cling to an idealized image of the past. The hope for the millennium is almost invariably rooted in the belief in an aboriginal golden age. Thus, in most religions, the joys of kingdom come are a replay of the lost paradise. Also political utopias often hark back to a lost primitive harmony. In therapy, we often see our clients reaching for a future that embodies the past as it "should" have been. The present can hardly compete with this imaginary past or with its twin, the "promised future." Therefore, the present is devalued as being in a state of decay; nostalgia and hope color the past and the future with marvels, but at the price of making the present drab.

Rigid hopes can wreak havoc also after people are disappointed. People who cannot outgrow the loss of a promise that, in their minds, embodied the whole meaning of existence, may have their life blighted by the carcass of a dead hope. The prototype of this condition is Miss Havisham, the self-immured lady in Charles Dickens' *Great Expectations* (1985). Miss Havisham lives in a house in which all clocks always display the same hour in a day long past. Sunlight is kept out of the rooms. She wears a bridal dress that has long grown faded. Her decrepit bridal veil is crowned by the specter of dead flowers. Everything has been left as it was at the awful moment when she was forsaken and left at the marriage altar. Miss Havisham does more than arrest time and block out the world. She hates life. Her blasted hopes have been transformed into endless brooding on revenge. She ends by being burnt alive in a fire that is ignited by her bridal dress.

But can we view Miss Havisham as suffering from hope disease? Is she not the obvious victim of the loss of hope, for whom the instillment of new hope would be the only possible medicine? She is. However, it is one of the characteristics of a diseased hope that it will not leave room for a healthier hope. Miss Havisham cannot renounce that ardent moment in which her life should have been exalted into absolute bliss. The hope was killed, but the acute intensity of the bridal moment fills her and warps her. The world that denied her ardent wish is ardently cursed. In effect, the old hope has not vanished but has been subverted into the black hope of revenge, which is infinitely more blinding, rigid, and mindless of sacrifice than almost any other hope in existence.

Following the lead of the masters we have identified with the tragic view (e.g., Epicurus, Epictetus, Montaigne, Spinoza, Schopenhauer, and the Buddha) Comte-Sponville urges us to relinquish our rigid hopes. "The work of despair," as he terms this inner endeavor, is the precondition of happiness.[3] This seems puzzling, because despair is a word with a purely negative connotation. For this reason, other thinkers in this tradition have usually opted for other terms to indicate the release from the bondage of diseased hopes (e.g., the Epicureans' *ataraxia* or the Buddhists' *nirvana*).

---

[3]The title of his major work is *Treatise of Despair and Beatitude.*

Some have come closer to Comte-Sponville and proposed terms like *creative hopelessness* (Hayes, et al., 1999). Others have even coined a new word, *inesperance* (in French, *inespoir* instead of *desespoir*). Comte-Sponville justifies the grimmer expression, *work of despair*, with the argument that before reaching the positive state of freedom from diseased hopes, one must first work hard to let go, which always entails a sense of loss. To speak of a leap into happiness without a preceding work of despair would thus be an illusion. The higher one's hopes, the more they rigidify and strike root in the mind. Hopes that are grasped with moderation would never make anyone diseased. However, once an extreme hope succeeds in gripping one body and soul, it will not give in to polite requests. All one's strength is then needed to break free from its bonds, to become detached, to "de-hope" (from the French *desespoir*). Comte-Sponville stresses that the word "despair" evokes the grim determination that is often required to pry a tyrannous hope loose from the soul. We shall remain content, however, with the less radical term, *work of disillusion.* Although we agree with much in Comte-Sponville's analysis, we would rather not aim at totally eradicating anything from the soul, not even a diseased hope.

CASE 21

Iris and Adam came to therapy because of endless fights, characterized by vicious mutual accusations. For almost a year there had been no physical intimacy between them. Adam complained that Iris never helped him in the management of the house and never showed him any civility, to say nothing of respect or affection. Iris felt persecuted by Adam's attempts to dictate to her how she should behave. He never stopped ordering her about and criticizing her behavior. His criticisms had become gradually more and more offensive. He taunted her with being slovenly, spiteful, hateful, destructive, and mentally ill. She felt that any compliance or sign of weakness on her part would only aggravate Adam's domineering and disqualifying stance. They humiliated each other before friends.

Adam believed that, deep inside her, Iris still loved him. In the past, she had told him that she loved him more than herself and that if something ever happened to him she would die. He was sure these feelings were still alive. Iris could not stand Adam's unshakeable certainty that he was always right and that she was to blame. She said he felt unconditionally entitled to her body, service, and love. His certainty of her underlying love seemed to her the utmost in offensiveness. For her, the marriage he dreamed of would be the most abject servitude.

Besides a weekly meeting with the couple, the therapist also saw each spouse individually. It turned out that Iris had always felt a physical aversion to Adam. All she wanted from the marriage was that they continue to bring up their child (parenting was the only area where Adam and Iris expressed some approval of each other) and that he leave her alone. She should not be obliged to talk to him when he came home. Every now and then Iris would raise the possibility of divorce, but would invariably stop short of any actual steps. In the aftermath of a particularly acute crisis, the therapist encouraged her to meet with a lawyer. She did so and decided she was not ready for divorce. Adam's declared goals were the opposite of Iris's; he would never divorce her and a cease-fire would not satisfy him. He wanted to improve the marriage in a positive way—he wanted friendship, respect, and physical intimacy.

Although the individual sessions were helping each spouse achieve his or her personal goals apart from the marital area, the therapist felt that the couple sessions had become turf for marital jousting. His therapeutic suggestions were being turned upside down, supplying fuel to the couple's arguments. The two were veering dangerously close to physical violence. A knife and a pair of scissors were brandished in one of the fights. The therapist feared he might be contributing to the negative spiral; he brought the case to a group consultation.

A major issue that concerned the group was whether the marital (as opposed to the individual) therapy should be continued. Six months of bi-weekly meetings had only served to make the spouses ever more intransigent. Therapy, by its very nature, fosters hope; maybe that very hope was fueling the couple's anger and frustration. After a lengthy discussion with the group, the following message was formulated by the therapist and read to the couple in the session:

> I want to share with you my thoughts about you as a couple, openly. I was not sure, until now, whether I should speak my mind in full, so I asked for a professional consultation. I became convinced that I would be harming you if I tried to "sweeten the pill."
>
> I think that you live in a mutual hell. You cause each other endless suffering. Your wishes for each other are deeply destructive. You, Iris, wish from Adam that he not *be*. You want him not to speak, not to ask, and not to desire. No act of his is acceptable to you. His mere presence insults you. You, Adam, would like Iris to be someone else; she should be a friendly, cooperative, warm, helpful, and loving woman. These are not negative wishes, but they are not Iris. Since Iris will not be the person you wish her to be, you try to prove to her that she is not only wrong but also evil, perverted, and sick. You want her to acknowledge herself as such. You both stay together because you fear the hell of divorce, which to your minds, might make the present hell small in comparison.

I cannot tell you whether this fear is unfounded. For the moment, I can only acknowledge the fear and the fact that it is the fear that keeps you together.

Your life in hell is made worse by hope: the belief you have that the other might change, realizing his or her mistakes and becoming a better spouse, makes you both more cruel in your demands and more vulnerable to disappointment. Because of these hopes, you both continue to inflict your wishes on one another.

I have decided to stop our joint sessions. I believe that they do damage because they feed your rigid hopes for each other. Our joint meetings have only made you push harder in the direction of these hopes. I believe that what you need is the very opposite: You need to engage in a constructive "work of disillusion." Disillusion is not a passive process. You, Iris, must become disillusioned from the hope of bringing Adam into inexistence. You will never reduce him to silence, to apathy, or to absence. If you had your way, he would become a vegetable. You, Adam, must become disillusioned from the hope that Iris will conform to your ideas. She will never be the person you wish her to be. You must also become disillusioned of your wish to break her, to make her acknowledge her faults, and confess how right you were all along. If you had your way, she would hate herself to destruction. The work of disillusion consists in telling this to yourselves, again and again.

I believe this will help you, not by making your marriage more fulfilling, but by making the fire of hell burn lower. You may become softened in your destructive anger and torture yourselves less cruelly. You will also damage your daughter less. She may then perhaps grow up in a somewhat sad family, but not in a seething cauldron. Disillusion may lead you to recover your humanity at home. I know you apart as well as together, and I find it a great pity how the two of you, whom I have learned respect and admire as individuals, have become so awfully transformed into each other's hell.

The couple remained silent for a long while. They asked whether the therapist would be willing to renew the marital therapy in the future, and the therapist answered in the negative. There were a few more sessions with Adam and with Iris individually. The bitter fighting stopped. Sometimes they had sex together. They stopped talking about divorce and went about the daily business of managing the home in a smoother manner. This much the work of disillusion allowed them. They did not, however, become close or even pleasantly companionable. Maybe it would have been better if they had found the courage to divorce. They did not choose this option, however, and the therapist did not think he was entitled to or capable of pushing them.

Illusions of Self

Modern psychotherapy is a true scion of Western culture in its affirmation of individuality. *Privacy, separation, autonomy, self-realization,* and *self-definition* are unquestionably positive terms in psychological discourse, whereas *symbiosis, enmeshment, lack of differentiation, dependency,* and *other-directedness* are pejorative ones.

There is something deeply unconsoling about this system of values, for if the self is our all, failure and death are absolute catastrophes. This logic entails that we can only be saved from the bleakest anguish by our ability to deny. It is only by erasing from our minds what lies in store for us that we can go on living. And yet, we know that it is not so; most people learn to live and fail, to endure daily the curtailment of their selves, and even to die in a sufferable manner, without blinding themselves completely or being totally overwhelmed by pain.

It seems that we are wiser than our ideologies. We all know that the self is not the crown of existence. We could not go on living if we really believed it was. We all have experiences to the contrary, and we all enjoy, at times, the feeling that there is more to us than us. We do not have to dig deep or far to find all around us examples of such experiences, like the following two.

CASE 22

Marianne was terminally ill. As her situation deteriorated, she became very stressed by things that should have not been significant in comparison with her condition. She was worried by the fact that many of her students were still not provided for, that her research project would be botched up, and that her son would not receive the help he needed for his problems. One might think Marianne was immersing herself in worries in order to distract herself from her real condition, were it not for the fact that she not only talked about her death candidly, but also dismissed all pseudo-optimistic remarks from her surroundings, simply by saying that this was not the way she had chosen to die. In the course of one week, Marianne's mood cleared up considerably. She achieved this by "cleaning up her desk." She made arrangements for her students, got a donation to the university to buttress her research after her death, and found a good therapist for her son. Improving things for the time when she would no longer be there had thus a clear positive influence on her daily suffering.

CASE 23

Carol suffered from recurrent bouts of acute anxiety about her physical condition. She went repeatedly to doctors and would only calm down when the doctors subjected her to strict examinations. She described herself as a person who could never let go. On one occasion, however, she had a remarkable experience in the course of a summer trip with her sister (who was almost as anxious as Carol). The two hesitated before taking a ride on a ski lift. Carol decided to take the plunge, although her sister chose to stay behind. Carol described her minutes in the air as the most liberating experience she had ever had in her life. She felt that all the worries and hassles that kept her continuously "cramped" had vanished. She said: "I felt one with the landscape. This is a hackneyed phrase, but that is exactly what I felt."

> Such experiences are not rare. We can probably tell of similar events in our lives or in the experiences of people we know. These are daily manifestations of the overblown term *self-transcendence.* Perhaps this is similar to what we feel when we are hugged in our pain; it is as if we have somehow become more than just our small crying selves. The feelings of relief and elation that sometimes accompany near-death experiences tell a similar story in more colorful terms. People usually forget the fullness of these experiences as they become once again immersed in the demands of daily living. And yet, many who go through it say that it diminished their fear of death. Probably such experiences console us by giving relief from our illusions of self.

Acquaintance with the experience of self-transcendence may provide us with a consolatory life philosophy that may keep us silent company even though, in our daily doings, we may be guided by completely different ideas. In Thomas Mann's family epic, *The Buddenbrooks* (1994) we read about Thomas, the head of the firm and the family, who carries all the world's worries on his back. There is hardly a character in literature that is so haunted by his responsibilities. When to his endless worries and hassles, the pain of a difficult tooth extraction was added, he collapsed and died in the middle of the street. And yet, some years before his death, an event had occurred that had provided a dampening counterpoint to the strained notes of his life. Thomas had become acquainted with Schopenhauer's philosophy, in which a carefully reasoned denial of the independent reality of the self was presented. In reading Schopenhauer's massive consolatory text, Thomas was carried by a wave of relief; his haunted self dissolved in the text. For a few blessed days, Thomas was not afraid and did not feel driven. Though he could not always follow the intricate arguments in the book, he felt he knew what the philosopher meant. He promised himself to keep the book always at hand, never letting himself forget it, never going back to his crazed "carousel" of worries. His life would change; he would not become trapped again. Near the end of the reading, he put the book in his night-table drawer, telling himself he would soon finish it and then reread it, again and again. He never finished the book or read even one single passage again. The demands of life claimed him back and the book accumulated dust in the drawer. And yet, the consoling ideas stayed in one of the drawers of his mind. Thomas did not achieve the freedom of the sage, and continued to live as the driven person he was. However, he carried Schopenhauer's consolatory wisdom somehow in the back of his mind. As a second philosophy, as it were; as a book in the drawer.

This might seem very little. After all, Thomas had promised himself that he would change his life, which he obviously failed to do. And yet we do not think his experience was valueless. Consoling thoughts hardly ever dominate our consciousness. The French philosopher, Henri Bergson, once said that every philosopher had two philosophies, his own and that of Spinoza (probably the most consoling philosophy ever devised). Bergson's idea about a second philosophy echoes our own thinking. The tragic outlook that we have tried to describe in this book will seldom take full hold of a person's mind and heart. Only sages attain perfection. Most of us must lead our daily lives, and most of us will sometimes hate and sometimes demonize. And yet the tragic outlook may stay in one of the "drawers" of our minds, as a second philosophy, moderating, consoling, and, it is to be hoped, gathering less dust than the book by Schopenhauer in the night table's drawer of Thomas Buddenbrook.

References

Abrams, M. H. (1971). *Natural supernaturalism.* New York: Norton.

Alain (1985). *Propos sur le bonneur* [Remarks about happiness] Paris: Galimard/Folio. (Original work published 1928)

Alon, N. (1985). An Ericksonian approach to the treatment of chronic posttraumatic patients. In J. K. Zeig (Ed.), *Ericksonian Psychotherapy, Vol. II.* (pp. 307–326). New York: Brunner/Mazel.

Amir, M., & Kalemkerian, R. (2003). Run for your life: The reaction of some professionals to a person with cancer. *Journal of Clinical Oncology, 21,* 3696–3699.

Anastasi, A. (1982). *Psychological testing.* New York: MacMillan.

Axelrod, R. (1997). *The complexity of cooperation: Agent-based models of competition and collaboration.* Princeton, NJ: Princeton University Press.

Bandura, A. (1969). *Principles ofbehavior modification.* New York: Holt, Rinehart & Winston.

Bates, J. E., Petit, G. S., Dodge, K. A., & Ridge, B. (1998). Interaction of temperamental resistance to control and restrictive parenting in the development of externalizing behavior. *Developmental Psychology, 34,* 982–995.

Bateson, G. (1972). *Steps to an ecology of mind.* New York: Ballantine.

Bateson, G., Jackson, D., Haley, J., & Weakland, J. (1956). Toward a theory of schizophrenia. *Behavioral Science, 1,* 251–264.

Beck, A. T., Rush, A. J., Shaw, B., & Emery, G. (1997). *Cognitive therapy of depression.* New York: Guilford.

Blume, E. S. (1990). *Secret survivors: Uncovering incest and its aftereffects in women.* New York: Ballantine.

Bugental, D. B., Blue, J. B., & Cruzcosa, M. (1989). Perceived control over caregiving outcomes: Implications for child abuse. *Developmental Psychology, 25,* 532–539.

Bugental, D. B., Blue, J. B., Cortez, V., Fleck, K., Kopeikin, H., Lewis, J., & Lyon, J. (1993). Social cognitions as organizers of autonomic and affective responses to social challenge. *Journal of Personality and Social Psychology, 64,* 94–103.

Bugental, D. B., Lyon, J. E., Krantz, J., & Cortez, V. (1997). Who's the boss? Accessibility of dominance ideation among individuals with low perceptions of interpersonal power. *Journal of Personality and Social Psychology, 72,* 1297–1309.

Chapman, L. J., & Chapman, J. P. (1967). Genesis of popular but erroneous psychodiagnostic observations. *Journal of Abnormal Psychology, 72*, 193–204.

Chekhov, A. (1979). *Anton Chekhov's short stories*. New York: Norton.

Chirot, D. (2001). Introduction. In D. Chirot & M. E. P. Seligman (Eds.), *Ethnopolitical warfare: Causes, consequences, and possible solutions* (pp. 3–26). Washington, DC: American Psychological Association.

Cohn, N. (1957). *The pursuit of the millennium*. New York: Secker & Warburg.

Cohn, N. (1975). *Europe's inner demons: The demonization of Christians in medieval Christendom*. London: Chatto & Heinemann.

Compte-Sponville, A. (1984). *Traité du desespoir et de la beatitude (I)* [Treatise of despair and beatitude]. Paris: Presses Universitaires de France.

Dawes, R. M. (1994). *Psychology and psychotherapy built on myth*. New York: The Free Press.

de Shazer, S. (1985). *Keys to solutions in brief therapy*. New York: Norton.

de Waal, F. B. M. (1993). Reconciliation among primates: A review of empirical evidence and unresolved issues. In W. A. Mason & S. P. Mendoza (Eds.), *Primate social conflict* (pp. 111–144). New York: State University of New York Press.

Dickens, C. (1985). *Great expectations*. New York: Penguin.

Eidelson, R. J., & Eidelson, J. I. (2003). Dangerous ideas: Five beliefs that propel groups toward conflict. *American Psychologist, 58*, 182–192.

Forward, S. (1990). *Toxic parents: Overcoming their hurtful legacy and reclaiming your life*. New York: Bantam Books.

Fromm-Reichman, F. (1948). Notes on the development of treatment of schizophrenics by psychoanalysis and psychotherapy. *Psychiatry, 11*, 263–273.

Fustel de Coulanges, N.D. (1980). *The ancient city: A study of the religion, laws and institutions of Greece and Rome*. Baltimore: Johns Hopkins University Press. (Original work published 1864)

Ginzburg, C. (1991). *Ecstasies: Deciphering the witches' sabbath*. London: Hutchinson.

Ginzburg, C., Tedeschi, A., & Tedeschi, J. (1992). *The night battles: Witchcraft, and agrarian cults in the sixteenth and seventeenth century*. Baltimore: Johns Hopkins University Press.

Greenberg, D., & Witztum, E. (2001). *Sanity and sanctity*. New Haven, CT: Yale University Press.

Hayes, S. C., Strosahl, K. D., & Wilson, K. G. (1999). *Acceptance and commitment therapy*. New York: Guilford.

Hilberg, R. (2003). *The destruction of European Jews (3rd Ed.)*. New Haven, CT: Yale University Press.

Hoffman, L. (1993). *Exchanging voices: A collaborative approach to family therapy*. London: Karnac Books.

Jabbour, E. (1992). *Sulkha: Palestinian traditional peace making*. Shfaram, Israel: International Peace Centre.

Jensen, A. R. (1965). A review of the Rorschach. In O.K. Buros (Ed.), *Sixth mental measurements yearbook* (pp. 501–509). Highland Park, NH: Gryphon.

Jervis, R. (1988). Realism, game theory and cooperation. *World Politics, 40*, 317–349.

Kelly, G. A. (1955). *The psychology of personal constructs*. New York: Norton.

Kertesz, I. (1992). *Fateless*. Evanston, IL: Northwestern University Press.

Kohut, H. (1971). *The analysis of the self*. New York: International Universities Press.

Kohut, H. (1977). *The restoration of the self*. New York: International Universities Press.

Kramer, R. M., & Messick, D. M. (1998). Getting by with a little help from our enemies: Collective paranoia and its role in intergroup relations. In C. Sedikides, J. Schopeler, & C. A. Insko (Eds.), *Intergroup cognition and intergroup behavior* (pp. 233–255). Mahwah, NJ: Lawrence Erlbaum Associates.

Lake, D. A., & Rotchild, D. S. (1998). Spreading fear: The genesis of transnational ethnic conflict. In D. A. Lake & D. S. Rotchild (Eds.), *The international spread of ethnic conflict: Fear, diffusion, and escalation* (pp. 3–32). Princeton, NJ: Princeton University Press.

Levack, B. P. (Ed.) (1992). *Possession and exorcism: Articles on witchcraft and demons.* New York: Garland Science.

Levine, R. A., & Campbell, D. T. (1976). *Ethnocentrism: Theories of conflict, ethnic attitudes, and group behavior.* New York: Wiley.

Loftus, E., & Ketcham, K. (1994). *The myth of repressed memory.* New York: St. Martin's Press.

Mann, J. (1973). *Time-limited psychotherapy.* Cambridge, MA: Harvard University Press.

Mann, T. (1994). *Buddenbrooks.* New York: Vintage.

Miller, A. (1981). *The drama of the gifted child.* New York: Basic Books.

Moffitt, T. E. (1990). The neuropsychology of delinquency: A critical review of theory and research. In N. Morris & M. Tonry (Eds.), *Crime and justice* (Vol. 12, pp. 99–169). Chicago: University of Chicago Press.

Moffitt, T. E. & Henry, B. (1991). Neuropsychological studies of juvenile delinquency and violence: A review. In J. Milner (Ed.), *The neuropsychology of aggression* (pp. 67–91). Norwell, MA: Kluwer Academic.

Nesner, H. (1999). "Hexenbulle" (1484) und "Hexenhammer" (1487). ["The Witches' Bull" and "The Witches' Hammer"] In, G. Schwaiger (Ed.), *Teufelsglaube und Hexenprozesse.* [Belief in the Devil and Witches' Trials] Munich, Germany: C. H. Beck.

Nisbett, R.E., & Cohn, D. (1996). *Culture of honor: The psychology of violence in the American south.* Boulder, CO: Westview Press.

O'Connor, F. (1994). *A Good Man is Hard to Find.* (pp. 117–133) In *The Complete Stories of Flannery O'Connor.* London: Faber & Faber.

Ofshe, R. (1992). Inadvertent hypnosis during interrogation: False confession due to dissociative state: Misidentified multiple personality and the satanic cult hypothesis. *International Journal of Clinical and Experimental Hypnosis, 40,* 125–156.

Omer, H. (2001). Helping parents deal with children's acute disciplinary problems without escalation: The principle of non-violent resistance. *Family Process, 40,* 53–66.

Omer, H. (2004a). *Non-violent resistance: A new approach to violent and self-destructive children.* New York: Cambridge University Press.

Omer, H. (2004b, September). Non-violent resistance and victimized siblings. Paper presented at the 5th European Congress for Family Therapy and Systemic Practice, Berlin, Germany.

Omer, H. (2004c, February). Non-violent resistance in the treatment of battered women [in German]. Paper presented at the conference, Authority and Relationship, at Osnabrueck University, Osnabrueck, Germany.

Omer, H., & Alon, N. (1997). *Constructing therapeutic narratives.* Northvale, NJ: Jason Aronson.

Omer, H., Irbauch, R., & von Schlippe, A. (2005). Non-violent resistance in the school [in German]. *Paedagogik, 54,* 42–47.

Omer, H. & Rosenbaum, R. (1997). Diseases of hope and the work of despair. *Psychotherapy, 34,* 225–232.

Omer, H., Shor-Sapir, I., & Weinblatt, U. (in press). *Non-violent resistance and violence against siblings. Journal of Marital and Family Therapy.*

Orford, J. (1986). The rules of interpersonal complementarity: Does hostility beget hostility and dominance, submission? *Psychological Review, 93,* 365–377.

Perelman, C. (1982). *The realms of rhetoric.* London: The University of Notre Dame Press.

Pettigrew, T. F. (1979). The ultimate attribution error: Extending Allport's cognitive analysis of prejudice. *Personality and Social Psychology Bulletin, 5,* 461–476.

Reich-Ranicki, M. (2003). *Mein Leben.* [My Life] Munich, Germany: DTV.

Rieff, P. (1979). *The mind of a moralist (3rd Ed.).* Chicago: The University of Chicago Press.

Schaffer, R. (1983). *The analytic attitude.* New York: Basic Books.

Shapiro, F., & Forrest, M. S. (1997). *EMDR: Eye movement desensitization and reprocessing.* New York: Basic Books.

Sharp, G. (1960). *Gandhi wields the weapon of moral power.* Ahmedabab, India: Navajivan.

Sharp, G. (1973). *The politics of nonviolent action.* Boston, MA: Extending Horizons Books.

Shneidman, E. S. (1985). *Definition of suicide.* Northvale, NJ: Jason Aronson.

Spanos, N. (1996). *Multiple identities and false memories: A sociocognitive perspective.* New York: APA Press.

Spence, D. (1982). *Narrative truth and historical truth: Meaning and interpretation in psychoanalysis.* New York: Norton.

Stolorow, R. D., Atwood, G. E., & Brandchaft, B. (Eds.). (1994). *The intersubjective experience.* Northvale, NJ: Jason Aronson.

Sulloway, F. (1979). *Freud, biologist of the mind: Beyond the psychoanalytic legend.* New York: Basic Books.

Sundberg, N.D. (1977). *Assessment of persons.* Englewood Cliffs, NJ: Prentice Hall.

Szasz, T. (1974). *The myth of mental illness.* New York: Harper & Row.

Taylor, A. J. P. T. (1966). *The first world war: An illustrated history.* New York: Penguin.

Tolstoy, L. (2003). *The death of Ivan Illyitch and other stories.* New York: Signet Classics.

von Kleist, H. (1978). *The Marquise of O. and other stories.* New York: Penguin.

Watkins, C. E., Campbell, V. L., Nieberding, R., & Hallmark, R. (1995). Contemporary practice of psychological assessment by clinical psychologists. *Professional Psychology: Research and Practice, 26,* 54–60.

Weinblatt, U. (2004, February). Non-violent resistance as parent-therapy. Paper presented at the conference, Authority and Relationship, at Osnabrueck University, Osnabrueck, Germany.

Weinblatt, U. (2005). Non-violent resistance as parent-therapy: A controlled study. Doctoral dissertation, Department of Psychology, Tel-Aviv University.

White, M. (1989). Saying hullo again: The incorporation of the lost relationship in the resolution of grief. In M. White (Ed.), *Selected papers* (pp.29–36), Adelaide, South Australia: Dulwich Center Publications.

White, M. (1997). *Narratives of therapists' lives.* Adelaide, South Australia: Dulwich Center Publications.

White, M. (2000). *Reflections on narrative practice: Essays and interviews.* Adelaide, South Australia: Dulwich Center Publications.

White, M., & Epston, D. (1990). *Narrative means to therapeutic ends.* New York: Norton.

Wood, J. M., Nezwozki, M. T., Lilienfeld, S. O., & Garb, H. N. (2003). *What's wrong with the Rorschach.* New York: John Wiley.

Zweig, S. (1982). *Triumph und Tragik des Erasmus von Rotterdam* [Triumph and tragedy of Erasmus from Rotterdam]. Frankfurt, Germany: Fischer. (Original work published 1935)

Author Index

V

W

Z

Subject Index